THE
FIREPLACE
ELIZABETH WILHIDE

THE FIREPLACE
ELIZABETH WILHIDE

LITTLE, BROWN AND COMPANY
Boston New York Toronto London

To my mother

FIRST EDITION

ISBN 0-316-94094-1

LIBRARY OF CONGRESS CATALOG CARD NUMBER 94-76029
A CIP CATALOGUE RECORD FOR THIS BOOK
IS AVAILABLE FROM THE BRITISH LIBRARY.

DESIGNED BY DAVID FORDHAM
TYPESET BY HEWER TEXT COMPOSITION SERVICES, EDINBURGH

PUBLISHED SIMULTANEOUSLY IN THE UNITED STATES OF AMERICA
BY LITTLE, BROWN AND COMPANY (INC.),
IN GREAT BRITAIN BY LITTLE, BROWN AND COMPANY (UK) LTD,
AND IN CANADA BY LITTLE, BROWN & COMPANY (CANADA) LIMITED

PRINTED AND BOUND IN ITALY

OPPOSITE *Victorian fireplace tiles courtesy of Stovax Limited*

CONTENTS

CHAPTER 1

INTRODUCTION

❉❉❉❉

FIRE COMES FROM THE HEARTH;
LONG LIVE THE FIRE OF LOVE.

Traditional Catalan proverb, inscribed by Gaudí on Casa Vicens.

T HE FIREPLACE IS THE HEART OF THE house. For thousands of years it has been at the centre of human habitation, enclosing the life-sustaining fire, marked by the richest architectural and decorative embellishment artists and craftsmen could provide.

Today, despite central heating and all the domestic conveniences of the twentieth century that have deprived the fireplace of much of its practical role, we are reluctant to abandon this ancient focus, steeped as it is in symbolism and centuries of tradition. Boarding up a Victorian grate or bricking in an inglenook may have seemed good ideas to postwar *aficionados* of the contemporary life style, but appear more like sacrilege today. Over the past decade or two, we have come to appreciate that conserving architectural heritage is not merely a matter of preserving grand rooms in stately homes, but also means respecting and reinstating the original features of older, less exalted houses.

In new homes, too, a fireplace is one of the most sought-after features. Advances in technology have brought us smokeless fuels, closed fireplace systems that deliver heat extremely efficiently but cause minimal pollution, and even highly insulated prefabricated flues and fireplaces that can be installed fairly easily.

As we warm our hands by a crackling log fire or fall into a peaceful reverie watching flames dance in the hearth, we experience the same sense of companionship and security that sustained our ancestors. But it's comforting to know that we do not share the same degree of dependence. Out of the ring of our cosy fireside circle there are no savage animals to be kept at bay by the leaping flames, no chilly stone corridors or marble halls to freeze us to the marrow, no impenetrable darkness after nightfall. We have hot water at the turn of a tap, and when we roast chestnuts and toast bread or marshmallows on the fire, we don't have to rely on the same source to cook the rest of our meal.

OPPOSITE *Based on an interior depicted by Hogarth, this room in an eighteenth-century house in London's Spitalfields carefully evokes the atmosphere of the period. Set into dark panelling, the eighteenth-century fireplace has a cast-iron fireback; the simple wooden mantelshelf carries an array of suitably authentic objects.*

LEFT *'Home Sweet Home' by Walter Dendy Sadler portrays a cosily domestic scene from the nineteenth century, with a family enjoying festive celebrations. The identification of hearth and home is a powerful one, taken for granted in centuries past, but no less relevant today despite all the conveniences of technology.*

MESSAGES IN THE FIRE

WATCHING A FIRE INDUCES A dreamy, peaceful state of mind. As the flames leap in the hearth, cinders jump out onto the floor and sooty smoke wafts up the chimney, it is easy to see why fire has long been a means of foretelling the future and even predicting the weather.

★If the flames are pale-coloured, expect rain.
★If the fire is noisy, expect a storm.
★If the fire burns fiercely, there will be frost.
★If the fire falls over in the direction of someone, there will be anger.
★If the fire retreats to a corner, there will be separation.
★If sooty smoke hangs above the grate, a stranger will arrive.
★Round or purse-shaped cinders that jump from the fire mean money.
★Oval or cradle-shaped cinders that jump from the fire mean birth.
★Rectangular or coffin-shaped cinders that jump from the fire mean death.

It is small wonder that previous generations marked the place of the fire by framing it with elaborate surrounds, by commissioning the finest carvers, sculptors, artists and craftsmen to enrich it with a wealth of decoration. An altar, a temple, a shrine, a proscenium arch: the form of the fireplace has always suggested a gathering place of power. Housing the energy that fuelled existence, the home was the hearth; this fundamental equation was underscored by making the fireplace the focus of familial pride and riches. In the modern age, the fireplace is a window through which we can glimpse the past, and begin to understand just what it was like to live centuries ago.

As long as we have lived with fire, we have known its dangers. Its mysterious energy, so enhancing and yet so destructive, is commemorated in a richness of symbolism and mythic imagery as old as history itself. If the fireplace has always been treated with great decorative attention in celebration of its central role, at the same time there is an acknowledgement of the awe and fear that fire also inspires.

The association of the fireplace with the house begins with the first enclosed hearths – central fires built on the floor of great raftered halls. Like a bonfire built indoors, these central hearths provided heat for cooking, light to see by, warmth and comfort for medieval communities sheltering under one roof. Gradually, as the fireplace moved back to its familiar place against the wall, enclosed within the structure of the building, its importance was given architectural emphasis. By the Renaissance, the fireplace had become an integral part of the design of the interior, the vehicle for designers, artists and architects to express their adherence to classical principles or display the summit of their artistry and taste in a glorious centrepiece.

Most of us have some passing acquaintance with ordinary domestic fireplaces of the past two centuries. Yet even in that relatively short time, there is an incredible variety of styles, materials and levels of sophistication. Elegant eighteenth-century chimneypieces with delicate classical motifs; wide country inglenooks spanned by broad oak mantel beams; panelled colonial surrounds with neat painted pilasters; glorious Victorian marble edifices and cast-iron registers inset with luminous tiles; and cheery Edwardian grates with copper hoods evoke each successive period of design more sharply and concisely than any other feature of the domestic interior. From the rustic to the palatial, each has its own decorative story to tell.

In the modern interior, there is no need to be enslaved by the decorative conventions of previous ages. Old fireplaces acquire new impact as the focus for fresh design ideas; new fireplaces lend a crisp sense of definition in clean-lined surroundings. Nevertheless, as many have discovered, it is particularly rewarding to restore an old fireplace to its former glory or install an appropriate design in an original setting. The satisfaction comes from reviving one of the most important elements that contribute to the architectural character of the house. At the same time we are reviving much more than that; as we light a fire to dispel the gloom of a winter's afternoon or gather round a merry yuletide blaze on the darkest days of the year, we renew ancient traditions, bringing warmth and cheer into the heart of the home.

'Whatever lives is fire.' When the Swiss alchemist Paracelsus wrote these words in the sixteenth century,

he echoed an ancient belief. Since the dawn of time, fire has been venerated as the life-giver, but no one knows when or where the story of fire really begins. Some claim that it was in Africa, about a million and a half years ago, that the first deliberate use of fire was made; others believe that it was in Asia, nearly a million years later. What is clear is that Peking Man, who dates from 500,000 BC, was known to have made use of fire, and by the time of the Neanderthals, 75,000 BC, cooking had been discovered, which implies that a degree of expertise in lighting, controlling and preserving fire had also been acquired.

How the idea of fire first occurred to these early humans is another matter for informed speculation. Natural accidents, such as forest fires started by lava flows or lightning, may have provided a clue. It is equally possible that in the act of fashioning primitive tools and

THE YULE LOG

A N ANCIENT WIDESPREAD TRA-
dition in many parts of Europe,
the Yule Log is reputed to bring
fertility and good fortune to the household. It is a very large back log or back
brand, brought into the house on Christmas Eve and used as the foundation for a
new fire. Lit from the remainder of the
previous Yule Log, it is anointed, toasted,
carried round the room, ridden on and
sung to, depending on the particular re-
gion. Rekindling the fire in the depths of
midwinter is a powerful symbol of renewal,
far older than the ceremony of Christmas
itself.

OPPOSITE *'Christmas Dreams
by the Fireside' (Anon)
encapsulates the hypnotic
power of the living fire. The
fireside has been a place for
storytelling, contemplation and
reveries since time began,
casting its own magical spell
– as every child knows –
at Christmas time.*

weapons, fires may have been ignited accidentally and the experiment repeated as the advantages of light and heat were increasingly appreciated. Shaping sticks for spears and sharpening flints against each other are two basic operations that echo the two most ancient forms of fire-lighting – methods that either depend on friction or concussion.

The fire blazing at the mouth of the cave, warming the cold night air, lighting the darkness and keeping mar-auding animals at bay, proved a powerful ally in the struggle for survival. When it was eventually realized that food that had been cooked by fire was infinitely more palatable than it was when raw, human society had advanced its first few steps on the road to civilization and culture.

To the primitive mind, fire must have been astonish-ing and awe-inspiring, and not merely because of its considerable practical benefits. Around the ring of stones encircling the open hearth, the first humans found community – and magic. If fire could transform life, it could also destroy and harm. Furthermore, it was extremely difficult to coax into life. It is not surprising that in prehistoric settlements the fire-maker was often the priest.

Rubbing two sticks together until the first wisps of smoke appear, or striking sparks from stones to fan into flames, are far from easy procedures even to the initiated. Another universal fire-lighting method among early civilizations was to rotate the point of one stick in the hollowed side of another, a technique refined by North American Indians who drove the rotating motion using the string of a bow.

To circumvent these difficulties, early societies hit upon the simple expedient of never letting the fire go out. Somewhere along the line it was discovered that if the ash and charred embers were kept after the fire itself had died down, especially if they were kept covered, the fire could be revived again the next day quite easily by raking and fanning the smouldering remains. This cycle of death and rebirth was another source of wonder, encapsulated in the myth of the fire-bird or phoenix who miraculously rises again from the cooling embers of its own remains.

Fire-making did not become significantly easier for thousands of years. From the Middle Ages in Northern Europe, keeping the central fire going from day to day was good household practice, reinforced by conventions and superstition. Even as late as the nineteenth century

RIGHT *Alchemy, the forerunner of modern chemistry, originated in China and Egypt before the third century* BC, *but eventually reached the West in the early medieval period. A blend of mysticism, magic and experiment, the practice of alchemy involved the use of furnaces and stills, seen in this engraving of alchemists at work.*

there were cottages in rural England where the fire had not been allowed to go out for generations. A cold dead hearth was evidence of the direst poverty and misery; having to beg a light from a neighbour to restart one's own fire was ultimate proof of fecklessness and imprudence.

In early civilizations, communal fires, ceremonially fed with fuel, burned night and day to provide burning brands for individual dwellings. It was but a short step for fire to acquire religious and even political significance. Altar fires in temples from Egypt to Greece to Rome, sacrificial fires on top of Aztec pyramids, undying tribal fires, were all symbols of eternal statehood, devotion and cultural identity.

In the Greek city state the civic hall, or *prytaneum*, housed the perpetually burning communal fire, sacred to Hestia, goddess of the hearth. Here, visiting dignitaries were dined and entertained, an early example of the powerful association of hearthside with hospitality. Colonists venturing out to establish new settlements took fire with them from the *prytaneum* to begin life in a new place.

In Rome the most sacred shrine was the Temple of Vesta, goddess of domestic chastity. Vestal Virgins tended a fire which never went out, symbolizing the importance of the domestic hearth as the foundation of the Roman state. It is not surprising that the temple, established in 715 BC, was itself frequently destroyed by fire and often rebuilt. Vesta was venerated in the Roman home and had pride of place at the hearth, flanked by gods of property and the larder. The fireplace was the scene of devotional prayer, a shrine to the domestic gods, and a means for the ordinary citizen to affirm his allegiance to the State.

LEFT *Edmund Dulac's 'Alchemist' (1911) portrays the more disreputable side of alchemical pursuits. Alchemy's main aims were to discover the secret of immortality (the elixir of life), a universal medicine, and a means of transmuting base metal into gold, which these early scientists believed to be the purest of all metals.*

With the coming of fire, man had learned to fear the dark. To sun-worshippers, fire was the goodness of life itself, light, warm, pure and sacred. Stone Age man was buried with his flint and iron pyrite to light and warm his way in the afterlife. Norse gods lived within a realm of fire. Ancient Greek philosophers believed fire was the origin of the universe, while ancient Britons worshipped the tree as a temple of fire in a natural identification of fuel with what it was consumed by. The Old Testament image of the Burning Bush, in which God revealed himself to Moses, depicted fire's essential creativity and powers of regeneration. Fire was one of the four medieval elements, the study of which through alchemy and magic forged the beginning of science. Translated into modern terms, fire was energy, the engine of life.

In the modern world, light and heat come at the touch of a switch. The radiator heats up, the thermostat adjusts, hidden services and remote power stations provide for the daily convenience and comfort of millions. Yet the tradition of fire and all it represents remains. Less than a century ago, within the living memory of our grandparents, fire was still the centre of life. Technology may have moved on at a great speed since then, but these ancestral traditions are harder to let go.

CHAPTER 2

THE HEART OF
THE HOME

❋❋❋❋

T HE STORY OF THE FIREPLACE AND THE story of the house are inseparable. Home and hearth are intertwined architecturally, decoratively and, above all, technologically. There is a natural tendency, now that our practical need for the fireplace has faded, to concentrate on its impact as one of the key architectural and decorative features of a room. It is therefore easy to forget that a fireplace is built into the fabric of a house, that it determines the way an entire building is planned and constructed. Over the centuries, as the fireplace changed, so did the house around it: neither can be fully appreciated in isolation from the other.

Hearth and home have been inseparable ever since fire was brought inside, so much so that almost from the start

the presence of a hearth has been a convenient, if highly unpopular, index for domestic taxation. With this dependence on fire as a source of comfort came, inevitably, closer contact with its dangers and discomforts. A fire burning inside a building brings with it the ever-present risk of the structure itself catching light. Then there is the question of what to do about the smoke, not to mention the vexed issue of how to control ventilation so that the fire burns steadily without either going out or devouring fuel too quickly.

Contemplating a cosy drawing-room fire, with smokeless coals glowing cheerfully in a neat iron grate, makes such difficulties seem remote, but in the beginning of fire's long association with people's homes, these were major obstacles to be overcome. The need to resolve

OPPOSITE *The main room in a traditional 'black-house' on the island of Lewis, Outer Hebrides, was warmed by a peat fire laid directly on the rough stone floor. The fire, which was never allowed to go out, filled the air with sooty smoke that eventually filtered out through the thatched and turfed roof. Central hearths persisted in remote areas long after their disappearance elsewhere.*

LEFT *The medieval wall fireplace was an all-purpose affair, furnishing heat, light and the sole means of cooking. This scene from c. 1470 shows a woman tending a pot on the hearthside as a round-bottomed cauldron simmers away suspended over the log fire on a ratcheted chimney hook. Altering the distance of pot from fire was the only means of varying the cooking temperature.*

RIGHT A *Roman hypocaust in Conimbriga, Portugal, dating from the second century* AD. *Literally 'a fire chamber', the hypocaust was a system of ducting devised by the Romans by which heat generated in a central furnace could be distributed throughout a building. The system was much used in public baths.*

BELOW RIGHT *'View from the Olden Time' by Joseph Nash shows a Victorian impression of Tudor festivities at Penshurst Place, Kent, with a central fire laid on the floor of the Baron's Hall. The central position of the fire was an efficient means of warming large areas, but it generated a great deal of smoke and posed great safety risks.*

them provided the spur to technological improvements that altered the way houses were planned and used.

HEATING IN ROMAN TIMES

Early Roman fireplaces were simple raised hearths located in the atrium in the centre of the house, from where, since the atrium was open to the sky, smoke could escape easily. Later, the atrium became the main living area and a separate kitchen was located in a back room along with the hearth, either positioned in the centre or set against a wall reinforced with stone.

The earliest fuel was wood, which more often than not gave off dense smoke. Roaring log fires threw off clouds of this smoke, which irritated the throat and stung the eyes, and the problem was worse if the wood had not been properly seasoned. For this reason, the principal Roman fuel was charcoal. Early on, it was discovered that if the fire was lit outside and glowing embers brought into the room to heat it, there was less smoke. Charred wood, or half-burnt chips, could be used to feed interior fires in braziers, coincidentally providing consistent heat for grilling and cooking. In the kitchen, harmful fumes were drawn off by a hood over a wall flue.

Like many other Mediterranean and Near-Eastern areas where the climate is essentially temperate, the Romans had floor-level braziers or radiators to take the chill off rooms in winter. These consisted of iron pots ventilated with air pipes set into a hollow in the floor, under a wooden cover and rug. But the most startling Roman innovation was central heating, a development designed for the comfort of those occupying the northern reaches of the Empire. By the first century AD the Romans had devised systems of hot air heating whereby a central furnace located in the cellar (the hypocaust) heated air that circulated in lead pipes and was ducted at floor level or through vents in the walls.

Like many other achievements of the ancient world, such expertise was lost during the dark centuries of the Middle Ages. Roman heating systems were the exception to the generally slow progress of fireplace development, and after the fall of the Roman Empire it was many centuries before Europe approached the same level of technological sophistication.

THE CENTRAL HEARTH

In contrast to the warm and sunny Mediterranean around which ancient civilizations flourished, the climate of Northern Europe was inhospitable. Cold, dark and damp for months of the year, in these areas basic survival depended on fire. At the same time, such conditions meant that fires were especially hard to light and to keep going.

As with all primitive cultures, the early peoples of Northern Europe relied on open wood fires. Whether fire was first brought into huts to warm them, or whether the hut evolved as a way of enclosing and screening a fire, the two gradually became indivisible. Primitive hearths were nothing more than shallow pits lined with stones, around which cooking pots rested on larger stones close to the flames. Later, Iron Age huts contained central fires with andirons to support the logs (see page 28).

Saxon timber buildings, rectangular rather than circular, were home to animals and humans, all under one roof. The open hearth formed the focus of one half of the structure, the other being devoted to stabling, pens, fodder and food storage. The fire was lit on a stone slab or in a pit in the beaten earth floor, the smoke escaping as

best it could through thatch or rafters, under the eaves, through windows ('wind-holes') or a hole in the roof. Around this fire gathered the inhabitants of the house, cooking all their meals and bedding down next to its warmth. The air would have been thick with smoke and the pungent odours of roasting meat, and there was always the risk of the whole structure catching light.

The familiar pattern of the medieval hall house developed from this basic Saxon house plan, with the livestock and stored food gradually accommodated in separate outbuildings. A lofty, double-height hall formed the main living quarters, a great communal area where food was cooked on the open central hearth, meals were eaten and the lowest ranking members of the household bedded down for the night on pallets. A good example of the medieval central hearth survives in the Baron's Hall at Penshurst Place, Kent, the home of the

RIGHT *The fourteenth-century kitchen at Glastonbury Abbey has four massive corner fireplaces. Such kitchens, catering for large communities, were often built as separate structures to minimize fire risk and remove the intense heat and smoke from main living areas.*

Sidney family since the time of King Edward III. An air vent in the vaulted roof allowed smoke to escape from the fire blazing below in the great eight-foot hearth. By the thirteenth century, such air vents were covered with louvred turrets designed to allow smoke to escape but prevent rain from getting in. The turrets were square or eight-sided and sometimes magnificently decorated. At the other end of the social scale, an open-ended barrel might be used for the same purpose in a peasant's cottage.

The hearth in a medieval hall was generally located near one end. Behind it was a platform or dais where those of the greatest rank sat at 'high table', closest to the warmth of the fire and set apart from the muddy, rush-strewn lower floor, vividly termed the 'marsh'. Sitting so close to the fire could be uncomfortable, however, and from the thirteenth century firescreens were used as a shield from fierce heat. Iron andirons or firedogs, increasingly elaborate in shape, supported logs and spits to roast meat and fowl; bread was baked under metal covers to one side.

In large households, such as manors and abbeys, where great numbers of people had to be catered for, the smoke, heat and stench that accompanied cooking over open fires became unbearable. Thus, from the time of the Norman Conquest, cooking was increasingly undertaken in a separate room or even a separate building so that heat, smells and fire risk could be controlled more effectively, or at least kept out of the way. Stone firebacks, or reredos, helped to concentrate the heat of the fire.

Nevertheless, the central hearth remained remarkably persistent, especially in smaller houses and isolated areas. In the Scottish Highlands and Islands as late as the seventeenth century there were cottages still with central fires where smoke wafted out through the thatch, and often as not back in again. Even so, the central fire was an efficient way of warming a space and its inhabitants, without the external heat loss that wall fireplaces generally entailed, while in buildings constructed of timber and thatch, a central position was much the safest. It is not too fanciful to suppose that the ancient associations of the central hearth, cosy and familiar despite all its disadvantages, helped keep the tradition alive long after the wall fireplace appeared.

LEFT *An illustration from a fifteenth-century French calendar and book of hours shows a man warming his feet before a wall fireplace. In the background a stack of logs are visible, cut to length and seasoned ready for use on the fire.*

THE EMERGENCE OF THE WALL FIREPLACE

If it takes a real effort of the imagination to conceive of life around the central fire of the thirteenth- or four-teenth-century hall house, the wall fireplace of medieval castles and abbeys is an altogether more familiar feature. Yet, after it was introduced by the Normans in the eleventh century, the wall fireplace took quite some time to supersede the central hearth, and the two forms of fireplace developed in parallel for several centuries. One reason for this was that the wall fireplace was a characteristic of stone building, and stone was expensive and difficult to work. A greater number of wall fireplaces survive today not so much because there were many more of them, but simply because stone buildings are long-lasting. Those that remain come from a narrow band of society which regularly employed stone.

Conquering peoples such as the Normans built in stone both to defend themselves and to assert their might and authority, and their towering castles, often set high on hills, rose through several storeys. In the fortified two-storey Norman hall, the great chamber, and its surrounding apartments set in the thickness of the wall, were located on the upper level, not on the ground floor. A storeyed tower or fortified manor house that has wooden floors spanning stone walls cannot be heated by a central hearth, for obvious reasons. And central openings are out of the question when the roof is a battlement.

The wall fireplace in this initial form consisted of a fire built against a wall, rather than enclosed by it. The thick walls of these fortified houses were their greatest defence and any significant recess would have weakened them unacceptably. Accordingly, wall fireplaces consisted of hearth stones placed against an external wall, with a stone fireback as protection.

For all their building skills, the Normans did not understand the importance of the flue in keeping a fire ventilated. The first wall fireplaces, good examples of which are those at Castle Hedingham, Essex (*c.* 1130), had short flues through the wall thickness, ending in vent holes only a storey or two above. A hood projected over the hearth to collect the smoke; alternatively, the fireplace might be slightly recessed and lined with bricks, with the flue divided at the back wall to form two vents on either side of a buttress.

The earliest existing chimney in England dates from the twelfth century. Stone cylinders, constructed within the thickness of the wall and extending a little above the battlements, were a vast improvement on side-venting flues, for they allowed the fire to draw better and smoke less.

The first wall fireplaces in the timber-frame medieval hall house were not in the great hall, which continued to be heated by central hearths until the fifteenth century, but in the solar, a small upper room behind the hall. Leaving his 'hearth-men' or retainers behind in the great hall, the lord of the manor now began to retreat to the solar with his family to dine in private. The fireplace here was set against a side wall, with a sloping hood channelling smoke up to a chimney.

A similar arrangement was adopted when the wall fireplace eventually made an appearance in the great hall. A smoke hood, made of timber, plaster or clay and supported by ironwork, directed the smoke from the hearth, on the side wall below the dais, up to the rooftop opening. The hood itself projected into the hall by as much as four feet. Such a design represents the not altogether happy marriage of two different patterns of building. To provide enough heat for these cavernous spaces, the wall fireplace needed to span a great distance. Fuel was devoured at an exorbitant rate because much of the heat was lost up the chimney or through the wall. Whereas a central fire drew air in equally from all sides, the wall fireplace, especially those on a scale to heat a hall, literally sucked air from its surroundings, creating incredible draughts. Screens around doorways, coverings for glassless windows and heavy layered clothing helped to mitigate the effects.

In front of the fire, which warmed only half the number of people that could be ranged round a central hearth, the heat could be exceptionally uncomfortable. In addition to firescreens, such arcane means as wicker-work leg shields were adopted to prevent scorching. At

OPPOSITE *This early wall fireplace, which dates from 1189, at Penhow Castle, South Wales, clearly shows how fireplaces were built within the thickness of fortified walls. A massive oak beam supports the rudimentary opening. The decorative fireback and andirons date from a later period.*

RIGHT *This wall fireplace on the second floor of Tattershall Castle, Lincolnshire (1436–46), is a fine example of Tudor craftsmanship, with its crenellated top, four-centred arch and heraldic carving. The lower hearth is characteristically lined in thin bricks set in a herringbone pattern.*

OVERLEAF *The Dining Room at Montacute House, Somerset (1580–99), features a fine Elizabethan fireplace dating from 1599, the year the original house was completed, placed in its present position when the room was created in 1789. Typical of this period was the practice of incorporating the heraldic devices of the family within the overall scheme of the fireplace decoration in an elaborate display of wealth, power and prestige.*

the same time, the nether regions of the hall remained distinctly icy. From this point, the hall began to decline as a communal living area, as the attractions of smaller, better heated rooms became obvious to all. The wall fireplace both demonstrated the advantages of subdividing large spaces and made it possible.

Between 1300 and 1600 the stone-built wall fireplace in abbey, castle and palace underwent considerable development and for the first time became a focus for decoration. Gothic stonemasons embellished the corbels or projecting supports for hoods with designs featuring flowers, foliage and carved heads; grand fireplaces in palaces might be enriched with figurative paintings. At the height of the Gothic, fireplaces were recessed, with pointed arches and carved heraldic detail in the panels above: among the finest examples are the fireplaces at Tattershall Castle, Lincolnshire, which date from 1435.

Nor was the chimney itself neglected. Progress was made in chimney construction during medieval times,

with ornamental capping and crenellations helping to diffuse the wind and keep the rain out. Chimneys were also plastered or 'parged' inside to stop up cracks and prevent draughts; the traditional recipe for parging, a mixture of dung and a cowhair mortar, dates from this period. Fifteenth-century City of London fire regulations stipulate that chimneys must be built of stone, plaster or brick, although, like many other official edicts, these were largely ignored.

By the fifteenth century, as the manor house lost its defensive characteristics, the fireplace was increasingly recessed, with the back of the fireplace projecting beyond the house wall and tapering to a chimney. The wide availability of brick as a building material hastened this change and enabled the expensive stone fireplaces of the nobility to be copied in humbler surroundings. At the same time, the projecting hood was abandoned and the fireplace came to consist of a stone arch flush with the surface of the wall, its interior lined in brickwork.

·15·99·

PRO   FOCIS
ARIS ET

Up until Tudor times, little attention was paid to the area over the fireplace. In the early sixteenth century this space was usually panelled to match the rest of the room or occasionally picked out with a tapestry or heraldic shield. But with rising trade there grew an increasingly prosperous merchant class, and the fireplace became a focus for the display of wealth and family identity.

Gradually, these highly ornamented fireplaces, enriched with allegorical detail and a bewildering variety of emblems and symbols, began to show the influence of the Renaissance, spreading slowly from Italy throughout the rest of Europe. It was to be another century and a half before classicism was adopted as a thoroughgoing system of design in the northern countries; at this point, classical details were copied, often crudely, by local craftsmen and simply added to the established repertoire of designs.

Already the focus of every important room, the fireplace now gained even more prominence; the chimney-piece extended as much as twenty feet above the hearth, and every square inch was carved, decorated or painted in an exuberant display of wealth and confidence. Great Tudor and Elizabethan examples can be seen at Burghley House, Loseley Park and Charterhouse in London, all virtuoso displays of craftsmanship that combine heraldic emblems and scenes from battles and mythology with columns, caryatids, scrolls, mouldings, flowers and foliage.

While incredibly varied in material and decoration, the overall composition of such fireplaces was classically inspired, even if proportions were generally squat and detail heavy and overloaded. A pair of columns on each side of the opening (which was now rectangular) supported an entablature above which, also framed by columns or caryatids, was the overmantel. This was divided into panels featuring coats of arms, insignia, detailed scenes, strange beasts or portraits of family members, and was surmounted by another entablature. Stone, plaster, coloured marble, as well as brick and wood

PREVIOUS PAGE *The dining room at Sheldon Manor, Wiltshire, boasts a fine collection of early oak furniture. The simple stone Tudor fireplace stands out against the dark oak panelling; to either side of the hearth are painted figural firescreens.*

RIGHT *A virtuoso display of fine carving, the alabaster chimneypiece in the Great Hall at Burton Agnes, Yorkshire, was built by Robert Smithson. It has been described by Sir Niklaus Pevsner as 'the most crazily overcrowded chimneypiece of all England'. The central panel (1610) depicts the story of the wise and foolish virgins. The upper part dates from 1570 and the fireplace was assembled in its present form in 1762.*

OPPOSITE *This view of the Parlour at Montacute House, Somerset, shows the original Ham Hill stone fireplace, a massive chimneypiece made from warm-coloured stone quarried locally and used in the construction of the house. The fireplace surround is decorated with strapwork.*

where stone was unavailable, were common materials; detail might be picked out in glowing colour or high-lighted with gold. Family mottoes or moral maxims, known as 'posies', were often carved over the fireplace or round the frieze. The whole effect was one of con-spicuous consumption and flamboyance.

The Jacobean chimneypiece at Boston House depicts the sacrifice of Abraham. In the great hall of Charter-house, a salamander, a creature who supposedly lived in fire, is carved in the central panel, while the overmantel panels at Speke House feature all nineteen of the children of Sir William Norris. In the great hall of Burton Agnes, built by Robert Smithson who also built Longleat and Hardwick Hall, the alabaster chimneypiece carving shows wise virgins virtuously at work, contrasted with maidens dancing and singing in gay abandon.

Such examples represent the height of fashionable taste and luxury in a prosperous, outgoing age. But even in lesser circumstances, the fireplace was beginning to be decorated, with wallpaintings executed on the plaster-work of the chimneypiece, sculptured lintels and other embellishments. The chimney itself was not immune,

and the decorative brickwork of the shafts – in spiral, octagonal, zigzag and round patterns – added a special note of exuberance to the Elizabethan and Jacobean skylines.

From the first appearance of the wall fireplace in Norman times to the grandeur of the great Tudor designs, the fireplace had firmly established itself as the decorative focus of the room. With the gradual abandonment of the central hearth and the soaring halls it served, rooms shrunk to a more recognizably domestic scale. The wall fireplace, the first fixed point in the room, ushered in the beginnings of interior arrangement. Benches, those all-purpose forms of seating for hundreds of years, were now left in place by the warming fire, with tables set up as needed for taking meals in relative comfort.

Yet the central hearth was not entirely eclipsed. Absorbed rather than banished, it lingered on in small manors, farmhouses and humble cottages. Now enclosed rather than open on all sides, for centuries to come it could be found still blazing away at the heart of the house.

RIGHT *'Madonna and Child at the Fireside'* c. *1430 by Robert Campin (1378/9–1444), sets its subjects in a comfortable interior of the period. The Virgin is warming her hands before a log fire laid on a pair of firedogs or andirons in a characteristically high wide stone hearth.*

WOOD LORE

Until the great forests of Britain began to show serious signs of depletion during the reign of Elizabeth I, the principal fuel had always been wood. A few centuries of burning coal and several decades of modern central heating have been long enough for the ancient knowledge of this varied material to be all but forgotten. Those who relied on wood for heating, cooking and life itself knew the qualities and characteristics of different types, in different conditions, knew how to season timber and knew which form was best suited to a particular use. Next to food, firewood was basic to human existence. Both were fuels for life, as acknowledged in the old-fashioned phrase 'to starve with cold'.

The Ancient Britons worshipped the tree as the embodiment of fire's life-giving energy. As we might see a match in terms of its fire-lighting potential, rather than a short stick with chemicals on the end, so wood *was* fire.

The distinctions between species of tree and between timber in different conditions were quickly learned. All timber, once it has been cut, loses moisture to the surrounding atmosphere, a natural balancing process known as seasoning. Green wood, freshly cut and full of moisture, obviously burns badly, whereas wood stored under cover in relatively dry conditions for up to a year is infinitely more combustible.

There are certain exceptions. The best firewood of all is ash, its name no accident. Ash will burn with a hot, colourful flame in any condition, green or seasoned, and enjoys a special place in northern folklore as *Yggdrasil*, the tree of life. Close behind comes oak, worshipped by the druids and used as fuel for their altar fires. Oak will also burn when green. Both woods were used as fuel in the best households and, if properly handled, gave off hardly any smoke.

Applewood produces scented, coloured flames; beech burns evenly, and beech shavings and hawthorn were reputedly the best choice for heating bread ovens. Cherry, willow and hornbeam make good firewood and burn clear and bright. Chestnut needs to be kept under cover for at least a year; its roaring flame, exploding with sparks, made it the ideal choice for outdoor bonfires but less favoured inside.

But there were many woods which burned less well and these often became associated with misfortune and death, which is not surprising since they were so poor at sustaining life. Yew was the tree of death (its leaves are toxic). An East Anglian superstition held there would be death in a household within twelve months of yew wood being brought inside. Elder also invited death. Poplar burns very badly and has an unpleasant smell. Elm, the Norman hanging tree, was often hollow – a bad sign, since witches were thought to be hollow. Elm is a poor fuel unless cut up into small logs rather than split, but its 'coldness' and reluctance to burn made it a good choice for the 'back brand' or log against which the fire was built.

Most evergreens and all resinous woods are unsuitable for indoor fires. Never entirely consumed, they throw off thick, pitchy smoke and showers of sparks. Fir and birch were the fuel of the poor; having to burn green wood was also a sign of poverty. Burning resinous wood coated the interior of a chimney with a tarry layer that easily caught light; to clear this away, holly branches were dragged through on a rope.

An ancient inscription on an Assyrian furnace reads: 'Keep a good, smokeless fire burning.' Domestic fires had to be equally well tended and this was often the job of the most trusted servant. The special responsibility of the Norman firekeeper was to ensure that the fire burned 'clean'. To this end, firewood was chosen carefully, seasoned and half-charred on an outside fire before being brought inside to feed the hearth. The special characteristics of partly burned wood were well understood, as they had been in Roman times.

Logs burn quite differently from coal and demand a wide hearth. Since the earliest times it was appreciated that retaining a deep layer of ash was essential, to prevent too much heat being lost from the fire and allow the right amount of air to circulate. More importantly, charred or glowing embers bedded in ash can be fanned into life the following day.

To this end, the fire cover was devised, a metal or earthenware domed lid which kept embers smouldering overnight and incidentally provided a convenient means of keeping food and drink warm. The fire cover – couvre-feu, 'curfew' or 'nightcap' – was also a safety measure that prevented sparks shooting out of the hearth onto rush-strewn floors and causing accidental fires at night when the hearth was unattended.

The term for this utensil came to be associated with the enforced practice of ringing a bell at a given hour as the sign for fires to be covered and people to retire for the night. Although the prime purpose of such legislation was ostensibly to reduce fire risk, curfew has always had its political uses: the 8p.m. curfew introduced by William the Conqueror in 1068 had the added advantage of preventing English rebels plotting over their fires deep into the night.

The considerable efforts that went into keeping the fire going reflected the difficulties of fire-lighting, particularly in damp climates. Firepans or *basons* were used to carry embers from hearth to hearth or to borrow fire from a neighbour. To start a fire from scratch, it was necessary to create a spark by striking a flint or sharp-edged hard stone against a piece of pyrite, later to be superseded by a small piece of metal, the 'steel'. The spark ignited tinder, creating a small, smouldering heap which could then be blown into flame and used to light secondary tinder of wood strips, which was not so quickly consumed. Tinder had to be bone dry, well-aerated and easily burned. Dried moss and fungi, thistledown, feathers and charred linen rags were common materials, while pine cones, tree roots, holly and ivy were used for kindling. The entire procedure was highly laborious, unreliable and almost impossible to carry out in darkness.

Wood fires were built in a variety of ways but in all cases care was taken to ensure the logs lay close together so the fire kept burning. Generally, the logs were laid

COAL AND CATHAY

On his return from Cathay, Marco Polo noted:

THE BLACK STONES WHICH they dig out of the mountains where it runs in veins . . . burns like charcoal, and retains the fire much better than wood; insomuch that it may be preserved during the night, and in the morning be found still burning.

BRAZIER HEATING IN CONSTANTINOPLE

Lady Mary Wortley Montagu, writing to Anne Thistlethwaite, 4 January 1718, from Constantinople:

MOST FAMILIES HAVING HAD their houses burnt down once or twice, occasion'd by their extraordinary way of warming themselves, which is neither by Chimneys nor Stoves, but a certain machine call'd a Tendour, the height of two foot, in the form of a Table, cover'd with a fine carpet or Embroidery. This is made only of wood, and they put into it a small Quantity of hot ashes and sit with their legs under the Carpet. At this table they work, read, and very often Sleep; and if they chance to dream, kick down the Tendour and the hot ashes commonly sets the house on fire.

OPPOSITE The practice of burning logs continued in country areas long after coal had become the standard fuel in larger towns and cities. The simple wide hearth in the seventeenth-century timber-framed cottage of the poet John Milton, at Chalfont St Giles, shows an ornamented iron fireback and andirons fused with a log basket, with a kettle suspended from a chimney hook.

horizontally, supported by andirons or firedogs. It was also the custom to place a large, unsplit log at the back of the hearth to act as a fireback. This 'back brand' glowed with heat and gradually shrunk, at which point it was replaced. Alternatively, logs could be piled vertically, leaning together. As the fire burned down, a single log was added at a time, placed at the back where the heat was greatest.

Unlike coal, which needs to be regularly stirred and well-aerated to burn properly, wood burns better if it is largely left alone. The poker, so indispensable for separating coals, was not found beside the medieval hearth, neither were there any fenders, which were devised only when there was the need to stop live coals rolling onto the floor. The principal utensils or 'fire-irons' for tending log fires were a shovel and tongs. A two-pronged fork stoutly fashioned in iron was also used, but these became more common only with the advent of coal fires. A bellows, used to resurrect the flames while saving on lung-power, was a late addition; Tudor examples were richly decorated and inscribed with mottoes and rhymes.

The andiron or, more picturesquely, the firedog (*landier* or *chien de feu* in French) is ancient in origin and consisted of a horizontal iron bar with a foot at one end and a pillar at the other. Placed at either side of the fire, its chief purpose was to support the logs and keep them from rolling out of the hearth. Many andirons had loops to support cooking spits and the tops were sometimes shaped (the 'posset-dog') to carry a cup for warming a drink. Early wrought-iron examples were often boldly shaped, but from the beginnings of iron founding in the sixteenth century, andirons grew increasingly ornamented, incorporating rings, roses, shields, figures, cherubs and various grotesque forms. In keeping with the fireplace's strong association with family life and heritage, andirons were also used to display crests and family symbols. Lavish examples, embossed and incorporating silver or brass finials or ends, date from the sixteenth and seventeenth centuries, by which time spit-carrying was the function of smaller, plainer andirons ('creepers') set between the ornamental ones. Cardinal Wolsey had forty-seven pairs, some incorporating the motif of the cardinal's hat; Louis XIV had forty-two pairs, all of them in silver.

When the wall fireplace arrived, the back of the hearth had to be protected from the flames, especially when brick began to supersede stone as a building material. From the late fifteenth century, iron firebacks were used and, like the back brand, helped to concentrate the heat of the fire and reflect it back into the room.

Early medieval firebacks were made by pouring molten iron into a sand mould. Pressing a variety of small objects, such as shells, knives and compasses, into the sand created simple, low-relief decoration, which was set off

by a rope-pattern border. Later examples, made by pressing a carved wood panel into the mould, were more elaborate. Like the andiron, the fireback was an ideal place to display the family emblem, and coats of arms and initials transformed a utilitarian object into a symbolic artefact. Biblical scenes and commemorative designs were also used and, updating an ancient symbol, one seventeenth-century fireback displays a phoenix to signify the Restoration of the monarchy in 1661.

Charcoal, a by-product of wood-burning, was used to provide heating in rooms without hearths, just as it was in ancient times. Portable metal braziers, some on wheels, some superbly decorated, warmed smaller, flueless chambers or supplemented the central fire. Charcoal burns hot, without ash, smoke or smell, but it has its drawbacks: burning it in an unventilated room can result in a poisonous and even fatal build-up of carbon monoxide.

To make charcoal, a mound of logs is completely covered with turf except for a hole at the top, through which glowing embers are dropped to ignite the pile. Once the logs are alight, the fire is controlled so that the wood half-burns in as airless a state as possible. To produce a ton of charcoal it is necessary to burn four tons of wood, but the resulting fuel retains three-quarters of the original heating power. Efficient and burning at an even, high temperature, charcoal was also used for iron smelting. It was to provide charcoal for the medieval foundries of Kent, Sussex and the Forest of Dean that great stretches of heavily wooded countryside were laid to waste.

In Saxon times, most of England was covered in dense forest; people could cut as much wood as they liked, and there was little replanting. As early as the twelfth century, however, timber stocks were showing the first signs of

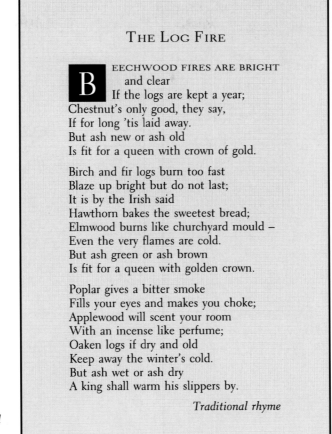

THE LOG FIRE

BEECHWOOD FIRES ARE BRIGHT
and clear
If the logs are kept a year;
Chestnut's only good, they say,
If for long 'tis laid away.
But ash new or ash old
Is fit for a queen with crown of gold.

Birch and fir logs burn too fast
Blaze up bright but do not last;
It is by the Irish said
Hawthorn bakes the sweetest bread;
Elmwood burns like churchyard mould –
Even the very flames are cold.
But ash green or ash brown
Is fit for a queen with golden crown.

Poplar gives a bitter smoke
Fills your eyes and makes you choke;
Applewood will scent your room
With an incense like perfume;
Oaken logs if dry and old
Keep away the winter's cold.
But ash wet or ash dry
A king shall warm his slippers by.

Traditional rhyme

OPPOSITE *This Dutch genre painting shows a kitchen interior with a servant girl at work beside a large fireplace with overhanging hood. Projecting hoods served to funnel smoke up the chimney. Just visible is a round-bottomed pot suspended on a chain and glowing in the heat of the fire.*

depletion and laws were laid down to restrict indiscriminate felling. Merchants had to pay a tax or *cheminage* to those in charge of the royal forests for the right to cut wood and commoners were not permitted to fell trees at all, although they were allowed whatever could be gathered 'by hook or by crook', such as branches pulled from the tree tops or fallen dead wood, the so-called rights of 'lop and top'. Dead wood and wood from permitted sources continued to be burned in country districts until well into the nineteenth century.

By the reign of Elizabeth I, regulations were in force to safeguard stocks of oak, ash and beech for shipbuilding, but land clearance for agriculture, house-building and, above all, charcoal-burning for iron foundries continued to consume native forests at a great rate. During the seventeenth century the number of trees in the Forest of Dean diminished by a third in under thirty years, while between the late sixteenth and late seventeenth centuries, the Forest of Arden completely disappeared. It became clear that a new fuel was urgently required. That fuel was coal.

CHAPTER 3

TEMPLES OF FIRE

E VER SINCE THE RENAISSANCE, THE fireplace has been an integral part of the design of the interior. Designers in the new classical manner revived ancient concepts of proportion and unity; the fireplace, no longer seen as a separate entity, was in scale and in harmony with the architectural detailing of the room as a whole. Some of the most palatial and artistically splendid chimneypieces date from this period but, on a less exalted scale, the rising middle class, with all its aspirations and refined sensibilities, has left an equally valuable legacy in the quiet dignity of the ordinary eighteenth-century interior.

The emergence of the fireplace as an architectural feature coincided with a change to a new fuel. Coal, which began to supplant wood as the main source of domestic heating in Britain, had its own impact on the design of the fireplace, requiring smaller openings, taller chimneys and different fireplace furniture. It also brought a pressing need for technological improvement which exercised some of the most inventive architectural and scientific minds of the day.

THE CLASSICAL VISION

Classicism, as a thoroughgoing system of design, was slow to reach Northern Europe from its beginnings in the Italian cities of the Renaissance, but once it gained ground in England in the early decades of the eighteenth century, conversion was swift and total. The classical vision swept all before it, affecting the design of almost every type of building and artefact. Fireplaces were no exception.

The architects of the Renaissance were guided by rules of classical design originally set out in the first century AD by the Roman architect Vitruvius. Central was the notion of the classical 'orders', of which the best known are the Doric, Ionic and Corinthian, used by both the ancient Greeks and Romans. Each order represents a blueprint for building design, consisting of vertical elements – the column, its base and capital – and horizontal elements – architrave, frieze and cornice, collectively known as the entablature. Rational, proportionally refined and, above all, flexible, the basic principle of the orders was applied not only to the elevation of buildings, but also to the

OPPOSITE *Kedleston Hall, Derbyshire, was designed by James Paine and built between 1757 and 1761, but it is more famous for the magnificent interior decoration carried out by Robert Adam (1728–92). The hall extends the whole height of the house and features 25-foot high pink English alabaster columns. The fireplace, with its plaster relief overmantel, is conceived as part of the overall scheme.*

THREE CHIMNEYPIECES.
DESIGNED BY JAMES GIBBS, ARCHITECT, IN 1739.

LEFT *Three designs for chimneypieces by James Gibbs, 1739. Gibbs (1683–1774) travelled widely on the Continent and studied in Rome. An important figure in the spread of Palladian ideas, Gibbs popularized the new style in his influential architectural treatises which were used as pattern books by builders in England and America.*

RIGHT *Castle Mheer, Holland, was rebuilt in the early seventeenth century. The drawing room fireplace, with twisted columns and a heavy carved overmantel framing a painting, reflects the sober dignity of early Dutch style. At this time, the preeminence of Holland as a trading nation brought widespread prosperity to a rising middle class.*

OPPOSITE *A magnificent Baroque fireplace in Castle Twickel Delden, Holland. The white marble relief, 1737, is by Jan Pieter van Baurscheit. Despite the ornate curves of the design, the fireplace retains an appealing solidity. The interior is lined in blue and white Delft tiles, a characteristic feature of many Dutch fireplaces, while branched candle sconces are incorporated in the surround.*

interior and all its features. It was this system of design, which originated in the great temples of the antique world, that was to transform the domestic altar of the fireplace.

The fireplace as we know it today derives from a basic formula devised in Italy during the sixteenth century, in which the chimneypiece projects into the room, the fire opening is framed by a surround and the area above is the focus for ornamentation. Architects, who were beginning to emerge as a distinct group of professionals controlling the design of buildings, were particularly concerned with the fireplace since it was the focus of domestic life. By the 1630s designs for fireplaces were published in Paris and, by 1700, the French were importing complete marble fireplaces from Italy.

The pioneer of classicism in England is generally acknowledged to be Inigo Jones (1573–1652), who travelled in Italy with his patron, the great collector the Earl of Arundel. At this early stage, English craftsmen were largely unreceptive to the classical ideals which Jones embraced so fervently. Nevertheless, in palaces such as the Queen's House, Greenwich (1616), and in the great public rooms at Wilton, Wiltshire, the seat of the Earls of Pembroke, a new architectural style was born.

The Double Cube room at Wilton, designed to display a collection of Van Dyck portraits, includes a magnificent

chimneypiece, one of the first to be executed in white marble. Extending the height of the room, it has a painted and gilded wooden overmantel and, in pride of place within a rich, carved frame, is the Van Dyck portrait of the children of Charles I. Festoons of fruit carved in marble, statues representing Peace and Plenty, fluted Corinthian columns, swags, scrolls, crests and pediments make a sumptuous display of wealth and power.

The grandeur of this stately composition set a pattern for seventeenth-century British fireplace design. In fashionable circles, the fire opening was heavily framed in marble or stone, topped with a pediment; alternatively, the upper portion might be elaborately constructed in wood, with a central panel devoted to a painting specially executed to fit the space. French versions were generally more compact and graceful and less massive than their English counterparts and there was great concern to integrate the fireplace with the wall decoration. In The Netherlands, the chimney breast was cut back to form a hood over the hearth. The hood was supported by polished marble columns or brackets, its interior faced in delftware tiles.

The dissemination of pattern books and the influence of foreign craftsmen greatly improved native English skills after the Restoration. Sir Christopher Wren

OPPOSITE *This illustration of an eighteenth-century French bedroom provides a clear example of the way the design of the fireplace was integrated within the overall scheme of a room. The vast overmantel mirror, flanking panels of damask and the Rococo curves of the fire surround, form a single harmonious composition.*

LEFT *Clandon Park, Surrey, was completely rebuilt for Thomas Onslow by the Venetian architect Leoni between 1713 and 1729 in a superbly elegant Palladian style. This fireplace in the Great Hall, a refined composition in grey and white veined marble, is enriched with a fine carved relief by the celebrated sculptor Michael Rysbrack.*

(1632–1723), the towering genius of English architecture, also left his mark on fireplace design. Wren favoured a more discreet style, with the fireplace treated as only a slightly more dominant panel within the scheme of a panelled or wainscoted room. Simple, heavy bolection mouldings of stone or marble surrounded the fire, and the overmantel, rather than an elaborate, dominant superstructure, was merely an enriched form of central panel. Yet, what enrichment! Wren could call upon the talents of the most masterly wood-carver of all time, Grinling Gibbons, who could carve almost anything, from a feather, to a lace cravat, to the open pea pod that was his signature.

Wren fireplaces often had projecting mantels on which were displayed collections of china, in special sets or 'garnitures'. The fashion for such symmetrical arrangements of Chinese porcelain, or candelabra, often with a central chimney clock, originated in France, as did the vogue for adding small mirrored panels or 'landskip glasses' below the inset painting. The Wren fireplace in the King's private dressing room, at Hampton Court Palace, features superb Gibbons' carvings, a projecting mantel, and a mirror between the mantel and surround.

The sobriety of Wren's designs was widely influential and his taste for simplicity was echoed in many smaller houses. Bolection mouldings in stone, marble or wood surrounded the opening, while the panel above the fireplace was filled with a mirror or painting, set off by a frame or carving. But Wren's preference for fireplaces positioned across the corner of a room was greeted with less enthusiasm. Corner fireplaces made for awkward furniture arrangements and fewer people could warm themselves directly by the fire.

Theatrical and magnificently ornamented, the supreme example of English Baroque is the fireplace in the Great Hall at Vanbrugh's Castle Howard. The work of Italian craftsmen, it features gilded stucco decoration atop carved marble, a soaring construction entirely appropriate in scale and drama for its setting in the seventy-foot-high hall.

In England, a more austere form of classicism was adopted in the early eighteenth century by an élite circle

RIGHT *A corner fireplace in the small drawing room of the eighteenth-century Swedish manor, Hople Herrgård, has a stone mantel and a panelled chimneypiece fitted with a narrow rectangular mirror. The sofa is set back against the wall in the typical eighteenth-century arrangement.*

OPPOSITE *Built for the Comte d'Artois in the autumn of 1777, the little pleasure pavilion, Château de Bagatelle near Paris, was designed in the height of the new neoclassical taste. The large plate of mirror glass over the fireplace reflects the view from an open doorway in a rigorously symmetrical scheme.*

of aristocratic patrons, the most notable of whom was Richard Boyle, 3rd Earl of Burlington (1695–1753). Travels in Italy, which increasingly provided the requisite finishing touch to a gentleman's education, also gave the opportunity for firsthand exposure to the new design ideas. The exquisite villas of the great Italian architect Andrea Palladio (1508–80) and the exposition of his version of classical principles in *I quattro libri dell'Architettura* (*The Four Books of Architecture*) had a tremendous impact on the aristocratic visitors who, upon their return to their native shores, wasted no time in commissioning classical villas of their own.

William Kent (1686–1748), who worked under the patronage of Lord Burlington, was an important figure in the transition between the full-blown extravagances of the Baroque and the calm rationality of Palladian classicism. At Holkham Hall, Norfolk, he tailored the design and material of each chimneypiece to suit the scale and importance of the room. White marble indicated the

best rooms, a convention that held for the next century and a half.

Kent's rather monumental chimneypieces generally incorporated an overmantel frame topped with a pediment, the so-called 'continued' style. If the central panel was not devoted to the display of a fine painting, it might be embellished with a classical medallion or sculptured panel, such as those created by Michael Rysbrack for Clandon Park, designed for the Earl of Onslow by the Venetian architect Leoni.

In France, by contrast, fireplaces were becoming lower and smaller. Mirrors now extended from the mantel right up to the ceiling. Lively Rococo frames were echoed in curvaceous surrounds which projected from the wall. The fireplace was seen as entirely integral with the wall and dictated its design: the dado was generally set slightly lower than the mantel, while wall panelling was taken to the same height as the central panel over the fire. Unity in decoration was the central innovation of the period, a

concept which originated in France, and the fireplace had an important role to play in determining the proportions of the room.

By the middle of the eighteenth century, the great expansion of trade meant that there was an ever more prosperous middle class eager to follow the aristocracy in matters of taste and fashion. Marble fireplaces were produced in workshops; pattern books showed variations in design that could be copied with increasing confidence and skill by architects, builders and craftsmen. Less expensive versions were produced in carved wood, which was then painted to look like marble or co-ordinated with the colour of the panelling or wall decoration.

In the form of pattern books and architectural publications the style was exported, crossing the Atlantic with early colonists. Colonial fireplaces in richer houses might have imported marble surrounds, but the chief characteristic of early American examples was simplicity. The fuel in this densely forested continent was, naturally enough, wood, which was also the main building material. Fireplaces were generally wide and rectangular, brick- or stone-lined, with plain wood surrounds and carved central panels.

Aside from the classical, more exotic tastes were also expressed in fireplace design. The asymmetries of the Rococo or the sheer whimsy of Chinoiserie, especially in

OPPOSITE *The Chinese Bedroom at Saltram House, Devon, features Chinese wallpaper and Chinese Chippendale bed and chairs. One of several fashionable mid-eighteenth century styles, Chinoiserie was often combined with classical architectural details, such as the fireplace in this room.*

LEFT *The drawing room at Womersley Hall in South Yorkshire has a fine plaster ceiling and fireplace, probably the work of the eighteenth-century architect James Paine. The fireplace opening is faced in Delft tiles and features classical mouldings, columns and medallions. On the mantelshelf is an appropriately symmetrical arrangement with a central clock.*

the hands of a designer such as Chippendale, transformed the fireplace into a setting of pure fantasy, while a taste for the Gothick could also be displayed in ogee curved surrounds.

Coinciding with the emergence of classicism in Britain was a boom in urban development. Speculative building transformed the appearance of London, Bath and other fashionable towns and cities, introducing the familiar Georgian square and terrace, with their neat, symmetrical elevations and elegant classical detail. John Wood the Elder, responsible for Queen's Square in Bath, noted that the new houses were fitted out with white marble chimneypieces, often as not surmounted

by handsome framed mirrors, in contrast to the old stone surrounds which needed constant – and messy – white-washing.

What we understand as Georgian style, however, owes much to the influence of one man, Robert Adam (1728–92). The second of four talented brothers, sons of a Scottish architect, he was the quintessential designer of his age. A student of Piranesi, he brought a new understanding of classicism home from his travels in Italy, derived from detailed studies of ancient ruins. Rather than the ponderous, sober character of Palladianism, which Adam scorned as 'absurd compositions', he introduced and immediately popularized

a lighter, more linear style, with a gracious, even pretty use of classical motifs. The new style, however, offended established guardians of taste and generated immense controversy.

The effect on the design of fireplaces was a return to the Wren pattern of doing away with the heavy chimney-piece enrichments and framing the fire opening more simply, the surround ending in a mantelshelf. The best Adam fireplaces were executed in white marble, with inlays of yellow sienna and verd-antique. Scrolls, foliage, urns, rams' heads, sphinxes and his trademark motif, the anthemion or stylized honeysuckle flower, were used with great delicacy.

The remodelling of Osterley Park, which Adam began in 1761 and finished nineteen years later, encapsulates the different periods of his work, an early boldness giving way to increasing refinement. In the Etruscan Room, the fireplace has a chimneyboard painted to co-ordinate with the wall decoration. Attention to detail was a characteristic of all

THE MOST EMINENT THING

Isaac Ware, from THE COMPLETE BODY OF ARCHITECTURE, *1754:*

WE ARE IN NOTHING LEFT SO much to the dictates of fancy, under the whole science of archi-tecture, as in the construction of chimney-pieces. Those who have left rules and examples from other articles, lived in hotter countries; and the chimney was not with them, as it is with us, a part of such essential importance. . . . With us no article in a well-furnished room is so essential. The eye is immediately cast upon it on entering, and the place of sitting down is naturally near it.

OPPOSITE *Robert Adam designed this white alabaster fireplace in the State Drawing Room at Kedleston Hall, Derbyshire, a room which overall represents one of the finest examples of Adam's work. The two large standing figures flanking the fireplace are a characteristic feature of Adam's early work. Adam was brought in to work at Kedleston by Sir Nathaniel Curzon (later Lord Scarsdale).*

RIGHT *Robert Adam was a master of detail. On occasion he is said to have sketched the type of landscape he felt appropriate when commissioning a painting from an artist. Adam collaborated with the finest craftsmen of his day. Thomas Carter created many marble fireplaces to Adam's designs. This detail is from a fireplace at Kedleston and shows Adam's mastery of classical motif.*

OVERLEAF *A Dutch castle is a fitting setting for this superb grey marble Louis XV fireplace with its sinuous Rococo curves. Pale straw yellow panelling highlighted with crisp white moulding and eighteenth-century furniture combine to create a period room with an authentic sense of elegance and delicacy.*

OPPOSITE *Belton House, Lincolnshire, was built in the late seventeenth century by William Stanton for Sir John Brownlow. In the Hondecoeter Room 'Dead Swan' by Jan Weenix is framed by elaborate giltwood carving, possibly by the Victorian restorer W. G. Rogers. The classical fireplace was installed under the direction of Lutyens (1869–1944) in the nineteenth century. To either side of the hearth is a fine 'famille verte' baluster vase.*

LEFT *A classical landscape by Francesco Zuccarelli hangs over the fireplace in the dining room at Saltram House, Devon. Robert Adam worked on the house in the late eighteenth century and first fitted out this room as a library. The plaster picture frame and fire surround display an acute balance of proportion and detail.*

Adam's work and it is not surprising that he concerned himself equally with the design of grates, fire irons and delicate fine pierced steel fenders.

The final phase of classicism began in the closing years of the eighteenth century, and lasted until industrialization and the beginnings of mass production in the 1820s marked the end of the era of craftsmanship.

A taste for antiquarianism and a new awareness of historical accuracy can be seen in the work of Thomas Hope, a leading figure in the neoclassical movement. The famous chimneypiece in his London dining room features a centrepiece bust by John Flaxman, celebrated neoclassical sculptor, flanked by an antique pair of horses' heads. Hope's strict adherence to Greek ideals was not to everyone's taste and was memorably ridiculed by Sydney Smith, who commented that Hope had 'brought two horses to his parlour fireside'.

Low mantels and almost minimal moulding were characteristic of the work of Sir John Soane, who took classical linearity as far as it would go. The severe, pared-down elegance of the Regency period was evident in simple marble fireplaces, with plain slabs forming columns, lintel and mantelshelf. Occasionally, gilt stars and spearheads, echoing Empire motifs, were used as

CLASSICAL CHIMNEYS

Sir Henry Wotton, from THE ELEMENTS OF ARCHITECTURE, *1624:*

ITALIANS, WHO MAKE VERY frugal fires, are perchance not the best Counsellors. Therefore from them we may better learn, both how to raise fair Mantels within the rooms, and how to disguise gracefully the shafts of the Chimneys abroad.

embellishment. Federal fireplaces in the new republic of the United States also showed the influence of French Empire. After the American Revolution, a neoclassical style after Adam gave way to more nationalistic emblems such as carved eagles, wheatsheaves and baskets of fruit on painted wooden surrounds.

During the seventeenth and eighteenth centuries, the fireplace had become a focus for the greatest artistic and architectural attention, expressing every variation of fashion and design. Few would disagree with the words of Isaac Ware, former chimney boy turned architect, and author of the standard eighteenth-century text, *The Complete Body of Architecture*. Writing of the chimney-piece, he said:

With us no article in a well-furnished room is so essential. The eye is immediately cast upon it on entering, and the place of sitting down is naturally near it. By this means it becomes the most eminent thing in the finishing of an apartment.

FIRESIDE COMFORTS AND DISCOMFORTS

Classical or Rococo, simple or richly ornamented, the fireplace remained the one element that made rooms habitable. Providing heat and much of the light after dark, the fire was the focus of social life. How the room was arranged and furnished reflected this basic fact.

Seventeenth- and eighteenth-century rooms were spar-sely furnished by today's standards, a minimalism accen-

OPPOSITE *The drawing room at Sir John Soane's museum (no. 13 Lincoln's Inn Fields, London) shows Soane's unique version of neoclassicism in the austere architectural detail, low relief moulding and brilliant use of colour. The classical fireplace is pared down to its bare essentials, complemented by a plain sheet of overmantel mirror.*

LEFT *Detail of a fireplace at Blickling Hall, Norfolk. Blickling is a fine Jacobean house by Robert Lyminge built on the site of an earlier house. It was extensively remodelled in the eighteenth century.*

tuated by the formality of interior arrangement, whereby furniture was normally placed against the wall when not in use. In the eighteenth century, much occasional furniture was designed to be portable, so that chairs could be drawn up to the fire or the window as needed, and tables set up to serve them. Formal sitting circles for conversation were grouped around the fireplace, but the fire also provided light and comfort for a host of other activities, from reading to sewing or writing letters. Pieces such as music stands, desks and worktables were also designed to be readily moved from place to place.

The cost of candles, especially those in finest beeswax, was prohibitively high, which increased reliance on the fire as a source of light. The convention of placing a

mirror above the fire has often been linked to the vanities of the age, when the display of personal finery was paramount. But mirror had its practical purposes, multiplying the effect of candlelight (as well as natural light) and creating a shimmering centrepiece for the interior. Polished metal fire furniture fulfilled the same function, glittering in the fire's glow.

Comfort, however, was not assured. Within the same room, there could be vast extremes of temperature, from the bitter chill of the furthest corner to the scorching heat of the fireside. Firescreens were an early device to protect the face from the heat of the flames. The first wickerwork screens date from medieval times, but the familiar framed panel on legs came in during the seventeenth century and

remained an indispensable accessory for two hundred years. Typical were carved or gilded wooden frames on tripod stands, with tapestry, embroidered silk or painted wood panels. The cheval screen was designed so that the panel could be adjusted to the correct position by sliding it up and down like a blind. The pole screen consisted of a round or piecrust screen that could be moved up and down on an upright pole fixed to a tripod stand. There were also hand-held, shield-shaped screens, delicately painted with figures. By keeping faces cool while the rest of the body remained warm, firescreens also ensured that complexions stayed pale and prevented facepaints from melting in the heat.

Typical Georgian ingenuity and care for comfort is displayed in the writing firescreen, a shallow panel on legs with a fold-down or hinged writing surface and compartments for writing materials. Eighteenth-century ladies were thus able to carry on their correspondence by the light and heat of the fire without ruining their complexions or becoming uncomfortably flushed. There was a slightly more robust model for gentlemen.

Panelled standing screens, too cumbersome and heavy to be moved with ease, helped to retain the heat of the fire within the sitting circle and block out the blasts of cold air that blew across the floor. The most expensive featured folding panels of lacquerwork or embossed

OPPOSITE *'Sir Lawrence Dundas and Grandson' by Johann Zoffany. Dundas, who made his fortune in armaments, was a patron of Chippendale and Adam and much concerned with matters of taste, as revealed in the walls densely hung with paintings and the mantelshelf arrangement of classical bronzes.*

leather. Another popular draught-protector was the high-winged chair that enclosed its occupant, shielding back and sides from the chilly room beyond the immediate hearthside.

Despite all these precautions, the temperature in many a fine drawing room or handsome apartment verged on

NUDITY AND THE FIREPLACE

Isaac Ware was concerned that classical fireplaces should nevertheless be modest:

MODERN SCULPTORS ARE FOND of nudities; but in a chimney-piece they would be abominable. [In polite society] some drapery is always to be allowed: the question is how much and in what manner.

the arctic. English houses were notoriously cold, the practice of heating homes with the more efficient Continental enclosed stove mysteriously never finding favour. Perhaps the English believed too firmly, in the words of Sir Henry Wotton (writing in 1624), that the sight of an open fire gave a room 'a kind of Reputation'. While new townhouses, with their sash windows, snug joinery and well-plastered surfaces, were undoubtedly warmer, those in the upper echelons of society, who enthusiastically adopted Palladian splendours, seemed oblivious to the discomforts of marble halls in a damp climate. A Swedish visitor to London in 1748 complained that the temperature in the drawing room of his wealthy host never exceeded 45°F.

The peripatetic life of the gentry, moving from town to country, or house to house, meant that rooms were often shut up for months at a time, with fires unlit. There are accounts of stairs, passages and back rooms running with water and hangings getting mildewed in the damp. Naturally, people relied on layers of clothing to keep

Maids of Honour Row, Richmond, Surrey, is a terrace of houses built in 1724 to accommodate the maids of honour of the Princess of Wales who lived nearby at Richmond Lodge. During the mid-eighteenth century no. 4 belonged to J. J. Heidegger, a theatre manager, who commissioned his scene painter, Antonio Jolli, to decorate the entrance hall. The panels show Swiss, Italian and classical landscapes in elaborate painted frames. In front is a figural screen – or 'picture board dummy' – a device often used to block off empty hearths in the summer; many were painted very realistically to resemble members of the family or the household.

OPPOSITE *The King's Hall in Skloster Castle, Sweden, which dates from the mid-seventeenth century, features a chimneyboard painted trompe l'oeil. Chimneyboards, which fit within the fireplace to seal the opening against draughts and downfalls of soot during the summer months, were often highly decorative, even whimsical.*

warm. In the early nineteenth century, one Lady Elizabeth Grosvenor kept warm with flannel underwear, two pairs of stockings and knitted 'muffetees' on her wrists.

Fireplaces posed different problems in the summer months when they were out of use, with wind, rain and soot pouring down the chimney and dirtying fine furnishings. The sight of a dead hearth was also discomfiting, and often a large vase, filled with flowers, was used to disguise the hole. A more practical and less cosmetic solution was to close the fire opening with a board or door of solid wood, metal or painted canvas stretched on a frame. The fireboard or chimneyboard was generally painted or papered to match the interior, or it might be decorated with a painting of flowers. A charming variation on this theme were figural screens, or 'picture board dummies', figures cut out of wood, with painted-on clothes and faces, supported by stands. These stood in front of the empty hearth in summer, and against the wall in winter.

In France, the great wood-burning château hearths were fitted with wooden or metal doors. The modern cliché of the lover escaping a husband's wrath by hiding in the wardrobe had its equivalent in early tales of the French court, where lovers similarly surprised took refuge behind the fireplace doors. An admiral sharing the affections of one of the mistresses of François I was nearly discovered when the King felt the need to relieve himself in the hearth (a common practice). A later scandal concerning a Parisian lady whose hearth was connected to a neighbouring house by a secret passage inspired a new toy – a cardboard hearth whose doors opened to reveal a risqué tableau.

KING COAL AND THE SMOKE DOCTORS

Coal has an ancient history. It was known to have been used as fuel in England before AD850. Marco Polo, returning from Cathay, noted that 'the black stones which they dig out of the mountains' burned like charcoal and retained heat better than wood. In 1239 the freemen of Newcastle were granted a charter to mine coal by Henry III.

For a long time, however, coal was the fuel of last resort, a sign of poverty and destitution. Undesirable because of the fumes and choking black smoke which resulted when it was burned in a hearth designed for logs, it was little used outside mining areas. The first supplies to reach London came by barge from the Tyne. Termed 'sea-cole' for this reason (to distinguish it from 'cole', which was the popular name for charcoal), it was banned in London as early as 1306. Elizabeth I forbade coal fires when Parliament was sitting; in 1580 she prohibited new building within three miles of London and sought to limit the

number of families – and thereby fires – to one per house. The desirable parts of London were soon established in the west, the direction of the prevailing wind.

There was no appreciation of the need for taller chimneys to take the smoke away and the polluted air of London was a grave cause for concern. This did not prevent great outdoor coal fires being burned during the terrible plague year of 1665, since the fumes were thought to act as a disinfectant, purifying the atmosphere and driving away evil vapours.

As the shortage of wood began to bite, there was, however, little choice but to turn to coal. Peat was an alternative fuel in poor or rural districts but it was too bulky to be transported very far. At first, coal was adopted hesitantly, even furtively, the persistent association with poverty making the better classes reluctant to admit to its

use. While a coal fire might do for everyday purposes, a wood fire was lit when visitors came.

Another factor which inhibited coal from being widely used initially was its erratic supply. In the years before adequate transportation, by canal, turnpike or – centuries ahead – rail, cities such as London had to rely on the colliers, plying their trade along the coast. Such sea routes were at the mercy of blockades by foreign fleets, which resulted in shortages and astronomical price rises. On 7 March 1667 Pepys recorded: 'This day was reckoned by all people the coldest day that ever was remembered in England; and, God knows! coals at a very great price!'

In 1634 sea coal was taxed, partly to restrict its use (the income made a significant contribution to the rebuilding of St Paul's). Then, in 1662, a new tax on hearths was

OPPOSITE *The saloon at Saltram House was remodelled by Adam between 1770 and 1772 and is thought to be one of his finest rooms. The walls are hung with damask and the chimneypiece, with red Brescia marble columns, is attributed to Thomas Carter the younger. The central relief panel depicts one of the Labours of Hercules. Flanking the hearth is a pair of pole firescreens.*

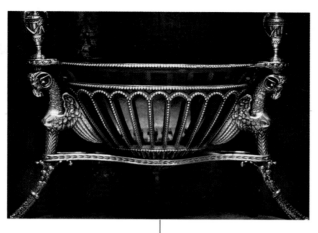

LEFT *This exquisitely detailed polished steel and brass gryphon fire basket was designed by Robert Adam for the fireplace in the Marble Hall at Kedleston. Basket grates fused andirons, basket and fireback in a single unit. The Adam brothers had a close association with the iron-founders, Carron Company of Stirling.*

imposed, reviving an ancient tithe. Like all forms of domestic taxation, this proved exceptionally unpopular and was repealed within a quarter of a century. Licensed 'snoopers', employed to detect untaxed hearths, fires or stoves, found as little favour as those who carried out the means-test of the twentieth-century welfare state.

Meanwhile, people were slowly learning to adjust to coal. A millennium or two in which to become well versed in wood lore had left them unprepared for the exigencies of the new fuel: in addition to its exceptional smokiness, it was hard to light. When the Woodmongers' Company transformed themselves into Coal Merchants, fire-lighting was part of the service offered to their new customers.

Coal also needed a constant draught of air from underneath to keep going at all. It was first tried out in the familiar charcoal brazier, but when such an arrangement filled the room with smoke, the brazier was moved to the hearth. The result was the first coal grates. Gradually, it was realized that both hearths and flues had to become narrower to accommodate the new fuel and, after the Great Fire of London in 1666, hearths were rebuilt to smaller dimensions.

Early grates were simple iron baskets that held the coals above the hearth. As coal became more socially acceptable, these evolved into the 'dog grate', where basket and andirons merged. There was no real need for andirons, of course, but this evocative feature of the wood-burning hearth was hard to abandon.

The 'basket grate' united basket, andirons and fireback in a single, self-contained unit. In this form, in the 1760s and 1770s, Adam produced beautifully decorated examples in polished steel. Such exquisite artefacts, in the words of historian John Gloag, demonstrated 'the Georgian designer's capacity for doing the right thing in the right way'.

In 1594 Sir Hugh Platt had established that a re-designed hearth, with false back and sides and a flue with a narrowed throat, was more suitable for coal. In 1624, Louis Savot noticed that unless a room had a through-draught, air would come down the flue and extinguish any fire, be it wood or coal; accordingly, he recommended a hearth reduced in height and width and a tapered flue. Old, wide openings were adapted by filling in with tiles or sheet metal.

The next development took account of such research and consisted of a built-in grate which enclosed the hearth and reduced its dimensions. The 'hob grate', which dates from the mid-eighteenth century and proved extremely popular, incorporated a basket flanked by enclosed boxed sides. The flat surface to each side of the basket made a convenient place to heat a cooking pot.

Fenders to prevent live coals rolling onto the floor and setting carpets alight had existed since the time of Henry VIII, who possessed the first recorded example. By the eighteenth century, fenders ranged from delicate and finely wrought affairs in pierced steel or brass rails infilled with wire mesh, to more utilitarian versions, wide and box-like, where pots could be set down to warm. Fire irons shrunk in scale and the poker became an indispensable fireside accessory.

RIGHT *This Regency fireplace at Normanby Hall, Lincolnshire, with its graphic use of contrasting marble and fine moulding, displays the linear quality of late neoclassical decoration. The rectangular mirror over the mantel is a characteristic feature of the period.*

OPPOSITE *Panelled walls painted sang-de-boeuf frame a simple eighteenth-century fireplace lined in Delft tiles in a house in Spitalfields. By the mid-eighteenth century most town fireplaces were adapted for burning coal, although the problem of fuel wastage and smoking chimneys continued.*

Coal was laboriously carried up from the cellar to feed the fires. One servant's manual instructed: 'Bring up none but large coals to the Dining-room and your Lady's Chamber; they make the best fires, and if you find them too big it is easy enough to break them on the marble hearth.' The same source recommends that chambermaids should oil the tongs, poker and shovel, not only to keep them from rusting, but to discourage 'meddling people' from stirring the fire and wasting fuel.

Since the seventeenth century, the idea of combining chimneys side by side in one stack had solved many structural problems, but the chimney was something of an eyesore to those eighteenth-century aristocrats and architects newly wedded to Palladian ideals. The classical villas that had inspired these country house builders originated in a gentle climate where there was no need for a roaring fire in every room. Chimneys represented an unhappy addition to the purity of classical façades and attempts were made to disguise them by hiding low stacks behind parapets or balustrades, or fashioning them in the form of Doric columns. At Mereworth Castle, Colen Campbell went so far as to conceal 24 flues between the two shells of the central dome. Smoke issuing from the top of a dome may have looked odd, but at least no chimneys spoiled the classical skyline.

Persistently smoky chimneys inspired many patent remedies. Smoke doctors offered their services, diagnosing individual problems and recommending cures. Chimneys were rebuilt time after time in an attempt to find a solution to this problem, which sorely afflicted many households.

Chimneys smoke for a variety of reasons. If the air at the top of the flue is at a higher pressure than the air below, a descending current will drive smoke into the room. A tall structure nearby, such as a tree or larger chimney, may cause the wind to rebound and divert it downwards. An unused chimney can draw in smoke from an adjacent flue. Poor lining, cracks or bends can spoil the draught, and cold flues smoke until the air has warmed sufficiently. Chimneys that are too large, too low or where the fire is insufficiently fed by air will smoke, as will those blocked by excess soot, birds' nests, leaves or other signs of neglect.

Chimney fires were a common hazard, especially if the flues had not been regularly swept. The chimney register, a sliding metal sheet that closed off the flue in the case of a chimney fire, dating from the mid-eighteenth century, was found to be highly useful at controlling the draught and survived as a feature of fireplace design throughout the nineteenth century.

Many of the attempts to perfect fireplace design were directed towards making more efficient use of fuel as much as reducing smoke inside. Prince Rupert, a nephew of Charles I, fitted an improved fireplace of his own design in his apartments. It had a low flue opening just above the fire and a hinged iron baffle that forced smoke down behind the fireback. The 'Bath fireplace' was an eighteenth-century variation of the hob grate, in which an iron plate over the fire reduced the flue opening. However, it set up voracious internal draughts, which quickly emptied small rooms of air.

European experiments with ducts, vents and valves, exploring principles of heat convection and reflection, generally resulted in constructions that were much too complicated and expensive for popular use. Benjamin Franklin, the American polymath who addressed the problem of smoky chimneys with the same enthusiasm as he made his experiments with electricity, invented various fireplaces, including one in which fire was contained in an iron vase and another which featured a revolving grate. His 'Pennsylvania fireplace' of 1745, an open stove designed for wood, was adapted for English coal-burning but proved too expensive for wide use.

A sad footnote to the story of coal is the plight of the chimney boys, the human casualties of this era of technological improvement. The old, wide, wood-burning flues had been readily accessible by ladder, and soot could be cleared by brushing and scraping, so preventing those accidents caused by the accumulation of debris. But the narrow flues demanded by the new fuel were not wide enough for adults to climb up them and, with cruel logic, children were sent up instead. Four- to seven-year-olds were ideal for the task, squeezing through constricted openings, round bends, into nooks and crannies, to clear the coal dust that silted on ledges and in crevices. Boys,

often stolen, were sold into slavery for this work and were regularly beaten and terrorized. The human toll was horrific: boys were sent up chimneys still on fire and suffocated in the heat; they fell to their deaths, or became trapped in the flues. But, blackened by soot, calloused and stunted, their knees and elbows rubbed raw on masonry, life was barely preferable.

This practice was tolerated and even sanctioned for more than 150 years. Those who controlled the sweeping trade had no desire to see their business transformed by 'machines' – jointed brushes – which required more supervision. Those whose crooked and poorly adapted flues would have needed to be rebuilt to accommodate new methods were in no hurry to spend the extra money. Legislation passed by the Commons was regularly thrown out by the Lords, whose large establishments would have required massive modernization.

It was not until 1875 that this barbaric form of child labour was abolished. *The Water Babies*, the famous story of Tom, the boy chimney sweep, published by Charles Kingsley in 1864, had a significant effect in turning public opinion.

CHAPTER 4

HOME FIRES

HE 'CHEERFUL BLAZE SO DEAR TO THE heart of every Englishman' remained the focal point of domestic life in the nineteenth century and right up to the First World War. The symbol of family togetherness, open fires now burned merrily in most rooms in the house, tended by a battalion of servants.

Fireplaces were produced in a rich variety of designs, as every conceivable historical period was revived in the medley of styles that characterizes the Victorian and Edwardian eras. Advances in technology, the growth of industrial production and the coming of the railway brought dynamic changes to society. Yet despite all the turbulent transformations to everyday life, one thing remained constant: the conviction that 'Home fires burn brightest.'

As the century drew to a close, reforms in grate design and flue construction, first envisaged a hundred years earlier, were put into practice. Homes were easier to heat,

fuel was cheap and more people enjoyed decent standards of comfort and domestic ease than ever before.

THE BATTLE OF THE STYLES

In the eighteenth century, classicism had provided a coherent ideal which united all aspects of design, from the ordered symmetries of townhouse elevations to the fashioning of a fireplace grate. Skilled craftsmen, working to pattern books, and often under the direction of an architect, helped to maintain the consistency and clarity which are the hallmarks of that era.

Industrialization brought irrevocable change. Mass production virtually spelled the end of the artisan and time-honoured techniques of craftsmanship in many different areas were quickly lost. The rapid expansion of trade and exploitation of colonial markets brought immediate prosperity to a burgeoning middle class. These new consumers of factory-made products dictated fashions through sheer spending power.

OPPOSITE *The Sherlock Holmes Room in a London pub is a reconstruction of a late nineteenth-century interior. The fireplace, with its arched opening and cast-iron grate, has accumulated a dense array of decorative objects on the mantel, which is trimmed with a valance.*

LEFT *This Yorkshire drawing room (c. 1838) was recorded by the amateur watercolourist Mary Ellen Best. While the decoration and arrangement is early Victorian, the room dates from the mid-eighteenth century and the fireplace, a conventional Georgian design, has a hob grate.*

VICTORIAN DISCOMFORTS

An account of winter conditions in a North-umberland house, mid-nineteenth century, by Barbara Charlton:

COAL AND FIREWOOD THEY had in great abundance, it is true, but the long passages had no heat, the outside doors were never shut, the hall and corridors were paved with flagstones, while to complete the resemblance of Hesleyside to a refrigerator, the grand staircase, also of stone, and the three large, old-fashioned, full-length windows half-way up with their frames warped by the excessive damp . . . contrived to make the downstairs space a cave of icy blasts. Even in my early years at Hesleyside funguses grew on the passage woodwork.

OPPOSITE *The massive neo-Gothic fireplace in the Winter Smoking Room at Cardiff Castle (1865) was designed by William Burges (1827–81) in a flamboyant mock-medieval style, drawing inspiration from French examples.*

Unlike the Georgian gentry, with their classical educations and Grand Tour sensibilities, Victorian merchants and professional gentlemen were not assured in matters of taste and, like all newly rich classes, nineteenth-century entrepreneurs tended to make up for lack of confidence with conspicuous display. The High Victorian clutter, which permeated every household by the latter part of the century, expressed status through accumulation of possessions, while providing a comfortable bulwark against the turmoils and tensions of a rapidly changing world.

The 'Battle of the Styles' was fought out on the domestic front, as past periods of design were plundered to add a gloss of luxury and borrowed glory to every artefact and interior feature. The fireplace was, as ever, the focus of much of this stylistic experiment.

First came a renewed interest in the Gothic. A playful, whimsical 'Gothick' style had been briefly popular in the eighteenth century, as a kind of fancy dress for buildings and furniture, but the early Victorian revival of medievalism, led by architects such as William Burges and A. W. Pugin, was made of sterner stuff. Advocates saw the

Gothic as the embodiment of Christian principles, a religiously 'correct' form of building. Great fireplaces were executed in the Gothic tradition by Burges, notably at Cardiff Castle, with fine stone-carving, painting and gilding. Neo-Gothic remained a significant force throughout much of the Victorian period, appearing in the detail of fireplace openings and surrounds in the form of crenellations, ogee shapes, pointed arches and other hints of medievalism.

Another mid-century revival harked back to a different age, the Merrie England of Good Queen Bess. Often there were Jacobean elements as well, hence the popular contraction 'Jacobethan'. Scottish Baronial, which Queen Victoria adopted for Balmoral Castle, and Troubadour (or *le style Henri III*) in France, betrayed similar aspirations. Large fireplaces with overhanging hoods, hunt trophies and collections of armour over the fire were associated (as was the Gothic) with masculine domains, such as the library or the dining room.

For the 'feminine' realms of boudoir and drawing room (gender distinction was prevalent in nineteenth-century decor) a version of eighteenth-century French Rococo –

OMNIA VINCIT AMOR ET NOS CEDAMVS AMORI

OPPOSITE *W. R. Lethaby (1857–1931) designed this towering marble chimneypiece (1883–88) which occupies the southwest corner of the Drawing Room at Cragside, Northumberland. It was the first house in England to be completely lit by electricity. At that time Lethaby was assistant to Norman Shaw, the architect of the house. It was built for Lord Armstrong, a millionaire engineer and dealer in armaments.*

LEFT *Victorian fireplaces were symbols of status, and shrines to traditional family values. This American polished marble fireplace in Victoria House, Portland, Maine, is characteristically elaborate. It was a common convention for fireplaces in drawing rooms to be white marble, whereas black or coloured marble was favoured for dining rooms.*

light, curvaceous, with gilt carving and plenty of mirror – was favoured on both sides of the Atlantic. The Louis Revival, blending elements of Louis XIV, Louis XV and Louis XVI, ranged from the Louis-Something versions of the mass-market to high quality reproduction and genuine antique articles in the homes of the wealthy. Antique collecting began in earnest in the early decades of the century, as a flood of fine French furniture came on the market following the French Revolution and found new aristocratic homes across the Channel. White marble fireplaces, with scrolling ornament, were designed to accompany this luxurious style.

Nor was classicism abandoned. Massive and sober Italianate designs, with pilasters and pediments, or lighter neoclassical styles 'after Adam', featuring urns and swags, remained popular, the linearity of Adam-style decoration proving easy to copy. Gothic, Tudor, Renaissance, Jacobean, Baroque, Rococo, classical – there was

scarcely an historical period left unexplored. To which may be added Moorish, Egyptian and Oriental, interpreted in varying degrees of accuracy and skill. By the 1870s, High Victorian eclecticism was at its peak.

During the course of the century, the planning and arrangement of interiors found the form with which we are familiar today: many different rooms, devoted to distinct functions and activities and with their own decorative conventions. Privacy was newly important, as was the segregation of classes under the same roof, whether in suburban villa or great country house. The home had become the sacred domain of the family, as distinct from a looser household of retainers, relatives, apprentices and other satellite members.

There were rules for fireplaces, too. The drawing-room fireplace was generally white marble. The standard version was quite plain, occasionally embellished, with thin, machine-cut lines that might be picked out in gold. The

dining-room fireplace was black, again of marble, sometimes with inset panels of coloured marble. Polished marble remained a popular material for fireplaces until the very end of the century. Bedroom fireplaces were smaller and less ostentatious than those in the best rooms and surrounds were often in a cheaper material, such as plaster. These distinctions were well understood and widespread. Speculative builders designated which room in a new house was to be the drawing room by the type of fireplace they put in and few new householders felt inclined to query their decisions.

Fire openings themselves were now often arched and completely filled in with black iron. In a small villa, the surround might be slate or painted cast iron or pine. Slate, in common use in the 1880s, was generally enamelled to resemble wood or marble; sometimes it was decorated with elaborate floral designs. A slate surround might also feature tiled panels in the flanks or 'cheeks', and decorative ceramic tiles in a range of brilliant colours and patterns were a feature of many late nineteenth-century fireplaces.

Cast-iron fireplaces of this date also had tiled reveals, or recessed sides, adding brilliant, jewel-like splashes of colour to the fireside. Cast iron was versatile material and could be moulded to follow all the stylistic vagaries of the period. Painted to look like marble or wood, or in

OPPOSITE *Oxburgh Hall, Norfolk, dates from the late fifteenth century. This exuberantly carved fireplace in the small dining room, with its facing tiles featuring the arms of the Bedingfields and Pastons, was introduced during the 1830s. The panelling in the room incorporates earlier seventeenth-century fragments.*

LEFT *This fire surround (1878) was designed by Thomas Jeckyll (1827–81), a leading figure in the establishment of Anglo-Japanese style design in the late nineteenth century. Jeckyll, an admirer of Japanese prints, made use of many Oriental motifs, notably chrysanthemums, cranes, butterflies and sunflowers.*

standard black, cast-iron fireplaces ranged from complicated designs for drawing rooms to simple bedroom fireplaces, with grate, canopy and surround cast all in one piece.

Above a wide mantelshelf of wood, cast iron or marble, was the obligatory overmantel mirror, which was framed in pine, gilded, painted or stained. Later versions were increasingly elaborate, with innumerable niches and shelves for the display of ornaments, mementoes and curiosities. The Victorians emphasized the importance of the fireplace with a characteristic density of decorative objects, natural history specimens under glass domes, vases and pieces of porcelain, as well as peacock feathers, fans and Far-Eastern artefacts acquired during the craze for all things Japanese.

There was also a tremendous amount of drapery. The mantelshelf was often concealed behind a mantelboard, like a pelmet, covered in flounced or draped velvet or thick plush and trimmed with ball fringing. Once the marble fireplace began to go out of fashion in the late 1890s, it too was often disguised with drapery. The overmantel mirror, often set in a velvet ground, might be framed in swags of lace and silk; even the fire opening itself might be flanked with curtains, drawn when the hearth was not in use. Where no armchair was without its

antimacassar, or piano without its shawl, the fireplace did not go underdressed.

The Victorian penchant for adding pantaloons to piano legs may seem to indicate a comically exaggerated sense of propriety, but it can equally be explained as a desire to conceal what was strictly functional. Home life was a refuge from the world of work, and the domestic interior, soft and enveloping, expressed this by relentlessly

HOT AND COLD

Extremes of temperature in the Victorian interior, noted by Mary Haweis in THE ART OF DECORATION, *1881:*

IT IS HORRIBLE TO HAVE A cold nose and a burning hand; it is more horrible to have a burning nose and cold hands. Fried toes alone are small comfort so is one hot ear, yet it is really not possible to be equally warm all round beside a fire.

PREVIOUS PAGES *Victorian interiors displayed a remarkable similarity despite the wide range of stylistic influences they employed. This comfortable drawing room at Rouse Hill, Australia, has the ubiquitous white marble fireplace infilled with cast-iron and a mantelshelf crowded with mementoes and personal treasures.*

RIGHT *Painted fireboards were a way of disguising an empty hearth in summer months. This charming floral bouquet sits in a nineteenth-century cast-iron grate, providing some protection from sooty downfalls and draughts, but rather more decorative interest.*

OPPOSITE A *magnificent carved fire surround at Leighton House, a studio house designed by George Aitchison for Lord Leighton in 1866. Aitchison also designed much of the furniture for the house in a mixture of historical styles.*

excluding any reminder of the practical realities of the outside world. Then, too, layers of drapery, trimmed and heavily fringed, were impressively luxurious and obviously expensive.

Both heating and lighting improved during this period and it was no longer necessary for furniture to be easily moved, night and day, summer and winter, to take advantage of the warmth of the fire or the rays of the sun. Furniture became fixed in position, with individual pieces heavy and solid. A central table, lit by oil lamps, was the focus of drawing-room activity, and occasional tables and chairs, informally laid out in conversation groups, thickly populated the room.

The fireside circle was no more, but the hearth remained the hub of cosy domesticity. Directly in front lay the hearthrug, usually shaggy, sometimes an animal skin. An 1888 guide for 'young householders' is predictably scathing on the home fashions of twenty years before. With wry amusement, the author recalls 'the woolly-bear hearthrug that always smelt of dust, and that was a receptacle for all sorts of cinders, toy-bricks, leaden soldiers, and bones dragged in and buried there by a delinquent dog or cat'.

Firescreens remained an invaluable accessory, but these, too, grew massive. Some incorporated collections of stuffed birds or specimens of butterflies, and were manoeuvred in front of the empty hearth during summer months. Coal grates, largely built in, could not be removed as easily as a pair of andirons or a free-standing basket grate and, when not in use, the standard advice was to hide the grate with a fan of pleated white paper or pierced brass. Decorative 'fire papers', fancy constructions in tissue paper, were widely popular as a means of disguising that unsightly, empty hearth. Alternatively, the space between fender and hearth might simply be filled with luxuriant potted plants, although how these survived the draughts and downfalls of soot is anyone's guess.

The club fender, with its padded top rail upholstered in leather, was a new addition to the fireside, particularly in the male regions of the house. Care was taken to co-ordinate the style and material of fire furniture with the style of surround; steel fenders and fire irons were the correct accompaniment of the white marble drawing-room fireplace. Behind the scenes, fairly substantial implements were employed to break up coal into manageable

HOME FIRES

74

WHAT TO DO WITH AN EMPTY HEARTH

Hints from J. E. Panton's FROM KITCHEN TO GARRET, *published in 1888:*

IN MY OWN CASE, AN OPEN Japanese umbrella suffices, because the temperature in England changes so quickly and so often that I scarcely can feel fires are an impossibility; but quite a pretty change in the room can be made by placing the sofa or the grand piano straight across the fireplace, of course removing fender, &c., and so making it appear as if it had vanished; while another nice effect is made with putting a fender made of virgin cork instead of the ordinary one, and filling up the grate with great ferns and flowering plants or cut flowers, frequently changed, for nothing save the ubiquitous aspidistra lives comfortably in this lowly and draughty situation.

OPPOSITE *Wightwick Manor, West Midlands, is a mock-Elizabethan house designed by Edward Ould for Theodore Mander and built between 1887 and 1893. The corner fireplace in the Oak Room is faced in decorative tilework which harmonizes with the soft tones of the William Morris fabrics used for curtains and upholstery.*

lumps, but at the hearthside all was refinement and gentility. For the best rooms, there were helmet-shaped brass or copper coal scuttles (or 'scoops'); another popular form of coal storage was a mahogany box with a lid, lined with galvanized steel. Coal breakers, decorative ash pans and the indispensable poker, with coiled, heat-resistant handle, often had brass details, imparting that essential showiness and glitter the Victorians prized.

It was matter of pride for the Victorian head of the family that the ladies of the household could languish in idleness or apply themselves only to the most genteel of pursuits. The gloom of the fashionable nineteenth-century interior owed less to technological inadequacies than the association of semi-darkened rooms, shrouded in thick drapery, with refinement and exclusivity. Firelight no longer provided the illumination for countless worthy tasks, but flickered in the hearth as a symbol of domestic virtue and propriety.

'We have a great Home, and its hearth is a Royal Woman!' Nothing could better summarize the Victorian identification of home, hearth, nation – and female virtue – than these words, written by an Ulster cleric in praise of Queen Victoria.

Reaction against the stifling clutter was inevitable. It first came in the form of the late-century Aesthetic Movement, whose aims, similar to those embraced by Arts and Crafts designers, was to restore 'art' and banish mass-produced mediocrity from the middle-class interior. The revival of the medieval inglenook by designers such as William Morris and Baillie Scott encouraged a new appreciation of traditional, rustic values (see 'The Rustic Hearth'). But as far as mainstream popular taste was concerned, the effect was to gradually lighten rooms, introduce softer, more natural colours and strip the fireplace of much of its enveloping drapery and fussy ornamentation.

RIGHT *Earthenware tiles created by the celebrated Victorian ceramics' designer William de Morgan (1839– 1914). De Morgan was influenced by Near-Eastern art and worked for a time in collaboration with William Morris. Tiles in glowing colour enlivened many late Victorian fire surrounds.*

OPPOSITE *This contemporary advertisement for 'Art Furniture' shows the effect of the Arts and Crafts movement on mainstream fashionable taste by the end of the century. The tiled and decorated fireplace is surmounted by a huge overmantel mirror.*

Wooden fireplace surrounds became popular, infilled with glorious tiles in either blue and white delftware or the luminous decorative work of ceramicists such as William de Morgan. Willow-pattern plates marched along the mantel, accompanied by Japanese fans and porcelain. Drapery fell from fashion and so did the marble fireplace. Those who could not replace such features (most homes were rented, which made large-scale alterations difficult), disguised them with paint. The general lightening and brightening of the interior coincided with an obsession with fresh air, sunshine and cleanliness as the necessary adjuncts of a healthy, happy life.

By the early twentieth century, creamy white woodwork was newly fashionable, and pine drawing-room fireplaces were often painted white, set off with plain green glazed tiles. There were also cast-iron 'Renaissance' examples. In the dining room, the fireplace might display panels of different coloured woods, while arched stone hearths, tiled grates and oak mantels struck a suitably serious note in the library. The standard Edwardian grate incorporated an iron or copper hood over the fire basket, while in the design of such details as fire furniture, the progressively minded householder kept abreast of new styles such as Art Nouveau.

Europeans had always found the stove more efficient than the fireplace, which tended to be treated as an architectural feature of the best rooms rather than a necessary accompaniment to everyday life. The corner fireplace was a feature of the early nineteenth-century bourgeois style, Biedermeier, a domesticated version of Empire style; but such an arrangement had never been popular in England, where the fireplace resolutely occupied the central position on a main wall. Even in the Biedermeier rooms of Northern Europe, however, the stove was a more common sight.

With a commendable practicality and desire for comfort in harsher climatic conditions, stoves had also become the preferred form of heating in the United States. During the nineteenth century, Americans experimented with prototypes of central heating, hot air or piped steam systems which relied on a basement furnace and a network of ducts and ventilating grates. In this age of industry and improvement, it was the English who clung to their open fires. English visitors to the United States often commented unfavourably on American heating arrangements. To such travellers, accustomed to freezing draughts and inefficient fires, American homes were far too dry and hot, the breeding ground of countless ailments and indispositions.

THE DOMESTIC ARMY

'As with the commander of an army, or the leader of an enterprise, so it is with the mistress of a house.' In these ringing tones Mrs Beeton set out to educate a generation in domestic economy. The organization of the home required such planning that there was a new need for instruction, particularly for the middle-class housewife who suddenly found herself with the perplexing task of running a large retinue of servants.

The open fire would not have lasted as long as it did in Britain were it not for the fact that both fuel and labour were cheap. Countries without a large workforce of servants, particularly the United States, were the first to investigate alternative methods of heating. But in

Britain, as long as there were chambermaids to sweep the hearth and light the fires, the old ways lingered on. It is estimated that 13 per cent of the working population of England and Wales were in service in 1851; by the 1890s, this figure had swelled to 16 per cent. Of the female population between 15 and 20 years old, an astonishing one in three were in service in 1891. Over the century, coal consumption soared from 10 million tons in 1790 to 240 million in 1900. The average house could store about two tons.

All these home fires were laid, lit and refuelled by young girls, underhousemaids, or 'slaveys' in the evocative contemporary term. The lowest of the low in the servant hierarchy, they did most of the hard physical

OPPOSITE *'The End of the Chapter' by Philip Wilson Steer (1860–1942). The open fire remained the principal source of heat in the Victorian home and British houses were undeniably chilly by our standards. Many Victorians believed warm rooms were unhealthy and an invitation to illness.*

work, even in households where there were also male servants. An 1863 cartoon showed a young maid struggling upstairs with a full scuttle of coal. Alongside is a strapping footman bearing his burden – a single letter on a silver tray.

Housemaids rose in the cold, dark dawn to begin the day's chores of sweeping out the hearth, blackleading the grate to prevent it from rusting, whitening the hearth, polishing up the brass fender and fire-irons, laying the fire, lighting it and disposing of ash and cinders. This punishing sequence would be repeated for each hearth, with countless journeys up and down stairs, carrying heavy weights of coal in one direction and full cinder pails in the other. When the mistress of the house awoke to her cheerful bedroom fire, or the master took his breakfast basking in the warmth of the dining-room hearth, the housemaid had already been busy at her tasks for several hours or more. As fires burned low, bell pulls hanging beside the fireplace summoned the maid to lay on more coals. Once a week, the flue had to be swept of soot.

Fire-lighting was the only part of the process which had improved significantly. Early experiments with gunpowder, phosphorus and chlorate had resulted in many explosions and injuries, but in 1855 the first safety match was made by a Swede, Johan Lundström, and matches became reasonably cheap in the second half of the century.

In new, terraced houses, the basement was the servants' domain. The front 'area', accessible by a door under the main stairs, was for tradesmen and deliveries. Coal was stored in a coal hole, or cavern under the stairs, its opening covered with an ornamental cast-iron plaque.

THE DUTIES OF A HOUSEMAID

Mrs Beeton gave this advice concerning the duties of a housemaid for daily fireplace cleaning and maintenance:

SHE SWEEPS THE DUST TOwards the fireplace, of course previously removing the fender. She should then lay a cloth (generally made of coarse wrappering) over the carpet in front of the stove, and on this should place her housemaid's box, containing black-lead brushes, leathers, emery paper, cloth, black lead and all utensils necessary for cleaning a grate, with a cinder-pail on the other side.

She now sweeps up the ashes, and deposits them in her cinder-pail, which is a japanned tin pail, with a wire-sifter inside, and a closely-fitting top. In this pail the cinders are sifted, and reserved for use in the kitchen or under the copper, the ashes only being thrown away. The cinders disposed of, she proceeds to black-lead the grate, producing the black lead, the soft brush for laying it on, her blacking and polishing brushes, from the box which contains her tools. . . . Bright grates require unceasing attention to keep them in perfect order. A day should never pass without the housemaid rubbing with a dry leather the polished parts of a grate, as also the fenders and the fire-irons.

One of the maid's tasks was to separate ashes from cinders, the ashes destined for refuse, the cinders going to stoke the kitchen fire. By the mid-century the kitchen fire had been transformed into the closed kitchen range, a logical progression from the hob grate with its enclosed sides. Like the open fire, the cumbersome range or 'kitchener' relied on sheer hard work to keep it operational. The fire box had to be cleaned out, ashes removed, oven cleaned, soot brushed away, hearth whitened and the entire monstrosity thoroughly blackleaded every day before the first kettle was boiled.

HINTS TO YOUNG HOUSEHOLDERS

J. E. Panton offered this advice on keeping the fire surround clean in her 1888 home manual:

A WOODEN MANTELPIECE CONtinues, as it were, the scheme of decoration of the room, and without being unduly prominent, makes the necessary unobtrusive frame for the fireplace that a staring white marble erection can never be. And . . . any stain from smoke can be washed off the painted mantelpiece, while a few days' carelessness, a smoky chimney, or a housemaid's unclean paws can ruin a marble mantelpiece beyond the hope of redemption. . . .

OPPOSITE *The kitchen at Wightwick Manor, little changed since 1888, is dominated by the huge black cooking range. Maintaining kitchen ranges was an arduous and backbreaking chore; fires were often kept going day and night, summer and winter, making for uncomfortable working conditions.*

Blackleading itself was laborious. A small piece of black lead (actually graphite) was broken from a block, mixed with water or turpentine in a little pan and brushed onto every iron part. When this had dried, the surfaces, including all the crevices, were rubbed with a special polishing brush, usually twice over. Polished steel parts of grates or stoves were kept bright with 'rotten-stone' (a cleanser made of decomposed limestone), oil and brisk rubbing with a leather.

Such relentless activity may be put down in part to the Victorian passion for cleanliness and concern for hygiene, which was a particular obsession in the last decades of the century. But there is no doubt that coal fires produce a great quantity of dirt and unless hearths are kept swept, the accumulation of ash will prevent the fire from burning properly. There was also a tendency to associate bad smells or 'vapours' with unhealthy surroundings, an assumption which was not unjustified in the days before proper drainage and sanitation. The kitchen range was the source of powerful cooking aromas at the best of times, but a range that was infrequently cleaned of grease emitted a rancid stench that permeated the house as a most unwelcome reminder of below-stairs life.

THE SCIENCE OF THE HEARTH

If Victorian homes gradually became warmer, it was largely because more rooms had fires and more fires were burned. The thick upholstery, layers of window drapery and carpeting must also have provided at least some insulation against draughts. Then there was the structure of the house itself. Most houses were built in terraced rows, with fireplaces on the party walls, a positioning which conserved heat within the construction. Each fireplace was required to have its own separate flue right to the top. The fire itself, however, was no more efficient than it had ever been and up to 80 per cent of the heat it produced was lost up the chimney.

What the Victorians considered comfortable and, more importantly, healthy, was rather different from modern opinion. Around 55°F was considered about right for the drawing room; a higher temperature, it was believed, brought increased risks of catching cold! Well-ventilated rooms were also vital for wellbeing. It was considered impolite for servants to close the door after leaving the room, a convention that encouraged those piercing through-draughts that foreigners found so uncomfortable. Since open fires require good ventilation to

keep burning, it is easy to see how the needs of the fire came to be identified with a healthy life style. The resistance to other forms of heating, by gas or electricity, when they eventually came in at the beginning of the twentieth century, rested on the notion that open fires were better for you.

Heat was not all that was going up the chimney. As the industrial towns and major cities became ever more populated and row upon row of terraces sprang up to cover green fields, billowing smoke issuing from innumerable chimney pots dirtied the air and just about everything else it touched. Coal smoke consists of the

unburned residue of gases, tar, ash and dust, and because coal is a relatively inefficient fuel, it is particularly smoky. The inefficient nineteenth-century grates exacerbated the problem – every time the fire was replenished with coals, it would start to smoke again and this smoke was pure fuel wastage.

By the nineteenth century London fogs were already legendary. Of course, these were not fogs at all, but smogs, thick sulphurous layers of polluted air. As transport improved, more and more families, in search of green fields and clean air, moved out to settle in suburban areas. The problem was not eradicated until the

deaths of four thousand people as a result of a single 'peasouper' in December 1952 led to the Clean Air Acts of 1955 and 1956, making it illegal to burn anything other than authorized 'smokeless' fuels.

The knowledge of how to improve the efficiency of the fireplace and control smoke had been available since the turn of the century, but no one made use of it. The man who had been responsible for solving these persistent problems was an extraordinary figure, Count Rumford (1753–1814).

Born plain Benjamin Thompson in Rumford, New Hampshire, Thompson nevertheless fought on the British side during the War of Independence. Political appointment in London, and the reorganization of the American Cavalry and the army of the Elector of Bavaria, were a few of his achievements. His interest in military catering led him to research ways of cutting fuel costs for cooking stoves, and he designed his own range, which made such efficient use of heat that supplementary hearths had to be provided to keep the cooks warm.

THE HEALTHY FIRE

From J. E. Panton's home manual, FROM KITCHEN TO GARRET:

FIRES WARM THE WHOLE house, take off the damp, raw feeling that is so trying in our English atmosphere, and gives a cheerful feel and look that cannot be too highly esteemed. I would rather do without any-thing than a fire, and even in the height of summer the instant it rains I have my fires set going, with the windows open, not so much for the mere warmth of course, but to dry the atmosphere and prevent the house-walls from becoming damp and dangerous to health; while for three parts of the year they are emphatically a neces-sity, unless we want the doctor's gig or brougham to be always turning in at our front gate.

OPPOSITE *This nineteenth-century engraving by Cruikshank shows a family displaying utmost consternation and alarm as a gentleman attempts to stir up the fire with a poker made of 'Britannia metal' – intended only for decoration. Showy or novelty fire implements were a common sight beside many Victorian hearths.*

RIGHT *'The Connoisseur' by Rowland Holyoake displays the ultimate in artistic firesides, with a suitably eclectic mantelshelf arrangement. By the end of the century, elaborate overtrimmed fireplaces were decidedly old-fashioned.*

RUMFORD'S REFORMS

Count Rumford set out the principles of fireplace reform in his essay 'UPON FIRE-PLACES', 1799:

T HE WHOLE MYSTERY . . . OF curing smoky chimneys is comprised in this simple direction: Find out and remove those local hindrances which forcibly prevent the smoke from following its natural tendency to go up the chimney. . . . Reduce the fireplace and the throat of the chimney, or that part of it which lies immediately above the fireplace, to a proper form and just dimensions.

BELOW *That age-old problem – the smoky chimney – is satirized in this 1846 cartoon: 'Beginning Fires for the Winter – Something Wrong with the Chimney'. The sweep advises: 'This chimley always was a bad un to smoke, sir; the party as lived here before you came had a deal of trouble with it.'*

Count Rumford (he received the title from the Elector of Bavaria in 1784) next turned his enquiring mind to the domestic fireplace. His research led him to the simple conclusion that the proportions were all wrong – the flue was too wide in relation to the fireplace opening and the fire itself burned too high up the chimney, where much of its heat was lost. He therefore proposed a narrowed flue, with a mantel opening set about 14 to 20 inches above the fire. The flue was designed with a constricted 'throat' or base, no more than four inches deep, to keep the fire from burning higher and promote a draught (this is still the standard throat size today). Behind the throat was a smoke shelf, which prevented soot or rain reaching the hearth and kept air circulating above, so that air was

not constantly drawn out of the room. The fireplace itself was brought forward into the room and fitted with splayed sides and back to radiate more heat outwards.

Rumford favoured firebrick for his construction, having established that polished metal does not reflect heat as well as dull surfaces. This may have been one of the reasons why his improvements were not widely adopted for decades: iron foundries had a lucrative trade in standard, cast-iron fireplaces, which were east to fit, decorative and cost only a few shillings.

'Rumfordized' fireplaces were installed in progressive or large establishments, notably the home of Lord Palmerston, and Rumford's research, published in his essay 'Upon Fireplaces' in 1799, won him many accolades in scientific circles. It is hard to understand why his reforms were not put into practice until nearly a century later.

In the meantime, Victorian inventors busily patented a wide range of devices designed to tackle one or more of the problems Rumford had already solved. There was a grate on castors that could be pulled forward into the room once the fire was going; there was a movable mantel that could be raised or lowered; there were 'hot air' grates which incorporated warming chambers, and even revolving grates which enabled fresh fuel, added at the top, to be rotated so that it burned from the bottom, avoiding the smoke that resulted each time a coal fire was stoked.

Despite all this ingenious effort, however, most grates in the middle of the century were still of the 'register' variety, where an iron fire opening, with hinged 'register' to control the draught, incorporated the fire basket in which the fire was laid. In some versions, opening, basket and surround were all of a piece.

In 1884, Rumford's ideas were finally taken up by Dr T. Pridgin Teale. Teale adopted the splayed sides and inclined back, faced in firebrick, of Rumford's designs and changed the arched opening to a smaller, rectangular one. His central innovation was the 'Economiser', a box under the grate with an adjustable air vent in front. The draught required to start a fire inevitably meant that, once it had caught, it would burn too fiercely, wasting fuel. Control from below enabled the fire to burn at a constant rate. As hot cinders fell into the box, they continued to burn down into ash; the fire literally cleaned itself, and could be left for half a day without attention. Needless to say, the ease and economies of Dr Teale's designs were popular and this type of grate was in wide use by 1900.

CHAPTER 5

THE RUSTIC HEARTH

✦✦✦✦✦

I N COUNTRY AREAS, FAR REMOVED from the fads and fashions of the town, life remained relatively unchanged for centuries. The old central hearth, enclosed and adapted, lingered on at the heart of the home, providing warmth, light and heat for cooking in small manor houses, farmhouses, and humble cottages.

The medieval inglenook, with all its connotations of fellowship, was a truly all-purpose fireplace, forming a room within a room where much indoor activity went on. It was this and other such traditional building patterns that inspired designers of the Arts and Crafts movement when they sought to replace the inevitable shoddiness of mass-production with a more craft-based aesthetic.

William Morris and his followers were among the first to express the keen sense of separation from the land that industrialization had brought in its wake. From the design of a wallpaper to the detail of a fireplace, their work was a reminder of that lost world in which man had enjoyed a close connection with nature.

In the dynamic and supremely technological twentieth century we are no less susceptible to such nostalgic yearnings and while it is undoubtedly easy to romanticize country life and ignore the hardships and privations of such an existence, an awareness of country traditions provides an invaluable sense of continuity with the past. This fascination with the vernacular has played a very real part in keeping the fireplace alive at the centre of the house.

THE TRANSFORMATION OF THE CENTRAL HEARTH

The central hearth, the oldest type of domestic heating, could still be found in remote cottages in something resembling its original form as late as the nineteenth century. By the fifteenth century, however, many central hearths in medieval hall houses were already being enclosed.

OPPOSITE *An English Renaissance stone fireplace, rescued from a demolished hall, forms the centrepiece in this North Yorkshire house which itself dates from 1450. The unusual brass andirons glitter in the fire's glow; wood stacked to either side of the fire basket dries out ready for use.*

LEFT *'The Clergyman's Visit' by Frederick Daniel Hardy shows an elderly couple receiving improving instruction from their clergyman. The wide inglenook, which occupies most of the cottage interior, has a window in the side wall and a chimney cloth to keep smoke from billowing into the room.*

RIGHT *'A Cosy Corner'*
(c. 1883) again shows the
impact of artistic reformers
on the design and decor of
ordinary houses. The built-in
seating recreates the effect of
an inglenook, while the
comforting motto 'East or West,
Home is Best' is inscribed over
the fire. A deep picture/plate
rail, dropped low around the
room, aligns with the high
mantelshelf.

OPPOSITE *The Dining Room*
at Cragside, Northumberland,
home of Lord Armstrong,
features the same worthy motto,
carved in the stone fire
surround. The inglenook
fireplace, designed by Richard
Norman Shaw in 1884, occupies
the entire wall and is fitted with
a pair of settles, stained glass
windows by Burne-Jones and a
richly decorative ceiling. The
carving is by James Forsyth.

Most houses that have survived from this and subsequent periods have undergone numerous changes over the centuries as successive generations, rather than starting again from scratch, made the additions, improvements and alterations necessary for their comfort and accommodation. Sometimes the front of the house was hidden behind a new façade to bring it up to date with stylistic trends – Tudor manors, for instance, were often 'upgraded' in the eighteenth century with the addition of a classically symmetrical elevation.

When a building has been progressively 'modernized', the fireplace can be an invaluable guide to dating the original structure. Blackened roof timbers at the upper storey are good indicators of the earlier presence of a hall, open to the roof and warmed by a central fire. A fireplace at the centre of the house plan, marked by a chimney in the middle of the roof, may also betray the previous existence of a central hearth, although some new houses built in brick in the sixteenth and seventeenth centuries retained the fireplace in this central position.

The first step in the transformation of the central hearth was the smoke bay. The smoke bay partitioned the hall vertically, enclosing the hearth within a single bay and helped to alleviate some of the smokiness of the interior. Within this timber structure, infilled with wattle and daub, meat could be hung and cured. At this stage, domestic animals were slaughtered yearly rather than overwintered, and smoked or salted meat and fish supplemented the diet in the lean winter months.

The smoke hood was the next development, a canopy of wattle and daub that hardened in the heat and funnelled the smoke out through a chimney-like shaft in the roof. 'Parged' inside with the traditional cowhair and dung, such structures were not fire-resistant.

By the sixteenth century, brick was becoming available for ordinary building purposes and the medieval hall house underwent further changes as brick chimneys were 'inserted' to enclose the old central hearth in fireproof surroundings. At this time, a floor was added halfway up the height of the hall to provide an upper storey and it was to this upper chamber that the family now retired, leaving domestics and retainers in less comfortable conditions below. The new chimneys were generally massive, sometimes occupying as much as half the hall, and incorporated two or more fires back to back, as well as fireplaces on the upper levels.

Despite these undoubted improvements, the enclosed fireplace meant that fewer people could directly warm themselves by the fire; the circle could not be completed. The answer was to incorporate seating as close to the fire as possible and create a room within a room – an inglenook or chimney corner. These broad hearths, with heavy oak timbers spanning the opening, might be large enough for a pair of benches or settles to flank the fire on

either side. Sometimes the whole recess was curtained off and windows might be built in the side walls. Often there were recesses within the chimney structure for smoking bacon or baking bread. The wooden mantel (sometimes a ship's timber) might feature simple carved decoration or be plastered in with the chimney breast.

In the first cottages with chimneys, these were built against the end wall, free-standing structures of the familiar wattle and daub or stone. Gradually, as building techniques improved and the sloping 'cruck' construction gave way to upright post and beam structures, the chimney was brought further inside, with three of its sides indoors. Eventually, just as in the hall house, the fireplace was at the centre of the cottage, dividing front from back, with the chimney forming a warm core at the heart of the building. Wide enough for everyone to

gather round, these inglenook fireplaces took up propor-
tionately huge amounts of space. Witch posts carved
with runic symbols to ward off evil were common features
of old inglenook hearths in country areas.

By the eighteenth century, the wall fireplace and
central hearth patterns had more or less merged. But
the central position of the fireplace was retained in
provincial terraced houses as late as the nineteenth
century, where each house had one double main chimney, with fireplaces back to back.

The rudimentary dwellings erected by pioneer settlers
in North America had chimneys at one end, made of
sticks and mud – as prone to catching fire as the timber-
frame wattle and daub constructions of medieval times.
Some settlers built their chimneys a foot or two from the

main log structure so that it could be toppled over away
from the cabin if it caught fire. Early fireplaces were little
more than holes in the wall; mantelpieces and surrounds
were often later refinements. In more prosperous colonial
homes, the wide kitchen fireplace extended the width of
the house, and was covered by a wooden hood to capture
smoke and greasy vapours. Inside the opening were hooks
for hanging pots and pans. In the south, kitchens were
often housed in a separate building to keep smoke and
smells away from the living areas.

THE ALL-PURPOSE FIREPLACE

The country fireplace was, as elsewhere, the focus of
everyday life. People gathered round the hearth to keep
warm and dry their wet clothing; they cured meat in the

OPPOSITE *'Expectation: the Interior of a Cottage'* by Frederick Daniel Hardy clearly shows how the inglenook fireplace was a room within a room. This example has a window in the rear wall; the fire is laid directly onto the floor of the hearth and there are branches propped to one side, presumably drying out for use on the fire. The indispensable bellows hangs on the facing wall to the right.

RIGHT *Another country inglenook, at Snowshill, is equipped with a range of cooking implements, including spits on a spitrack over the mantelbeam and various warming pans to set down on the fire. The high-backed settle and winged chair are traditional forms of seating that help to protect the back from draughts and keep the heat in the fireside circle.*

smoke, kept guns dry in racks on the chimney breast; they told tales and sang songs in the glowing firelight and, most importantly, they cooked on or beside the fire, and baked in recesses built into the fireplace walls.

The basic cooking implement of the medieval cottager was a cauldron, suspended from a tripod or by a hook or chain from an iron or wooden bar set across the chimney opening. The round bottom allowed even distribution of heat, and simmering inside, often for days and even weeks on end, was a brew of grains, beans, root vegetables, scraps of meat and the odd bit of game. The 'pease pudding in the pot, nine days old' of nursery rhyme fame was an approximation of the staple diet of North Europeans. The fire was not allowed to go out, nor was the pot often completely emptied, merely supplemented by whatever produce or fresh meat was to hand. This type of slow cooking made the best of basic foodstuffs and sinewy flesh, but it also reflected the fact that very little temperature control is possible when cooking on an open fire. In addition, there were skillets on trivets, long-handled pans and basket spits for roasting larger pieces of meat or fowl.

Sometimes the cauldron was used to boil up different foods at one time, each individually wrapped in linen bags or sealed in earthenware jars. The jars were held in place by a board with holes cut into it, wedged halfway down the cauldron. Early pioneers to the New World took their cauldrons with them, along with iron bake ovens and skillets on legs that could be set down on the campfire.

RIGHT *The romance of country firesides exerts a powerful appeal. This rudimentary fireplace, with overhanging hood and cobbled hearth, seems to promise long evenings of story-telling and reflection. Shoes and other tokens have been uncovered in the lintel or chimney where they were bricked up for good luck.*

OPPOSITE *The kitchen of a great nineteenth-century country house was a hive of industry from before dawn to well past dusk. Catering for large households and hordes of guests required a battalion of servants, even with such labour-saving devices as the hydraulic spit installed here at Cragside.*

The earliest form of baking in these simple surroundings was carried out beside the fire. Dough was placed on a griddle covered by a pot and glowing embers were heaped on top. With the wall fireplace, bread ovens were built into one side and shared the same flue as the open hearth. The oven was heated by brushwood or faggots, then the hot ashes were raked out, the bread dough placed inside, and the hot ashes banked against the door to seal in the heat. The even temperature which resulted was ideal for baking. Also set into the wall by the oven was a salt-box, where salt could be kept dry and readily to hand.

Quite elaborate methods were eventually devised to vary the distance of cooking pots from the fire and in this way provide at least some form of temperature control. The chimney crane was a vertical iron post, sunk into the hearth or hinged to one side. A horizontal bracket swung out over the fire, enabling pots to be exposed to different levels of heat. Kettle or pot tilters meant that kettles could be poured without burning the fingers.

Spit roasting was the favoured method of cooking meat. Indeed, the fact that the English have always been so keen on meat roasted in this way supposedly was another reason why they remained reluctant to abandon the open fire in favour of the closed range. Spits have to be turned constantly to cook meat evenly and it was the young and old who were often set this laborious task, protected from the blazing heat by screens of wet woven straw. In kitchens of great households, various means were employed to turn the spit mechanically using weights and gears; by the eighteenth century, it was rotated using hot air rising in the flue, harnessed by a 'smoke jack'. Few accounts of fireplace technology fail to mention one especially inhumane solution to the problem, which was to use small dogs, specially bred for muscle power, to run a treadmill.

With the advent of the hob grate, cooking vessels became flat-bottomed and legless. And gradually, during the course of the nineteenth century, in country areas as well as towns, the closed iron range became more

OPPOSITE *The fireplace alcove in the Hall at Wightwick Manor features William Morris upholstery fabrics and painted windows by C. E. Kempe. The embossed copper hood over the fireplace and the wrought iron and brass firedogs are handmade and thought to be by Morris and Co. The craftsmanship of these fireside accessories represents a challenge to the mediocrity of much Victorian mass-produced ironmongery.*

LEFT *This cast-iron stove, on display in a re-creation of a Victorian nursery, features decorative Minton tiles. A vast range of tiles were produced for use on fireplaces and stoves, from highly detailed pictorial patterns to simple natural flower or leaf forms.*

prevalent. But old ways lingered on longer in the rural hinterlands, and the open country fireplace, with all its traditions, was slowest of all to change.

INGLENOOKS AND COSY CORNERS

The England of yeomen farmers, medieval halls and manors, a true vernacular of architecture and craftsmanship dating back to the Middle Ages, was the tradition recaptured by William Morris (1834–96) and his followers in the Arts and Crafts movement. Previous Gothic revivals had concentrated more on re-creating the prestigious features of castles and cathedrals, rather than looking to domestic building for inspiration. But Morris had a different vision and believed that there were more basic principles to be learned. He understood, as many Victorian revivalists did not, that traditional forms must be adapted and applied with fresh appreciation by each generation: 'It is no longer tradition if it is servilely copied, without change, the token of life.'

William Morris is better known for his fabric and wallpaper patterns and perhaps even for his politics and poetry than for his effect on fireplace design. Nevertheless, in the context of Morris's lifelong campaign against what he saw as the debased products of mindless industrialization, the fireplace played an important role.

Red House, designed for Morris in 1859 by Philip Webb, is an early expression of his architectural and decorative beliefs. In the second-storey drawing room there was an open hearth overhung by a great brick hood rising up to the raftered roof. The brickwork was plain and unadorned except for the motto: *Ars longa, vita brevis* ('Life is short, art is long'). This powerful evocation of a forthright vernacular style was a radical departure for its day, when the typical drawing-room chimneypiece recalled Renaissance or Rococo splendours.

Another medieval form which interested Morris was the inglenook. The finest example of this is in the Great Parlour at Wightwick Manor near Wolverhampton. The inglenook fireplace which dominates one wall forms a sitting alcove, an enclave within the vast double-height room with its decorated timber roof and gallery. Richly decorated with tilework, woven hangings and murals, the inglenook displays the full range of the creative energies of Morris and Co. The inherent cosiness and charm of this traditional style had a significant effect on mainstream taste.

By the late nineteenth century, vernacular forms were beginning to attract renewed interest. Morris had railed against all kinds of showiness and fakery in the interior

PREVIOUS PAGES *The cheerful
day nursery at Wightwick
Manor was redecorated in the
1930s. The large fireplace and
sturdy wooden overmantel take
up a considerable portion of one
wall, the hearth screened by a
brass guard rail.*

RIGHT *Designed in 1861 for
William Morris by the architect
Philip Webb, Red House,
Bexleyheath, Kent, was a
startlingly original house in its
day, both for the simplicity of
its furnishings and the
forthright English vernacular
style of building. This brick
chimneypiece with its hints of
medievalism is in marked
contrast to the overblown
Victorian style of the period.*

OPPOSITE *M. H. Baillie Scott
(1865–1945), a contemporary
of Charles Rennie Mackintosh,
was much concerned with the
poor quality of design and
workmanship evident in late-
Victorian interiors. This house
in Switzerland designed by
Baillie Scott shows his rigorous
approach to design, coupled
with an enriching use of colour
and tile decoration.*

which obliterated the natural beauty of honest materials
and workmanship. He was horrified when Rossetti, the
co-tenant of Morris's country home, Kelmscott Manor,
disguised an old stone fireplace with a green faux marble
painted finish. It was the ultimate desecration. His
invective even extended to the obligatory Victorian array
of fireplace utensils at the fireside, a clutter of 'trumpery'
ashpans, pokers and tongs. Walter Crane commented on
how Morris had reintroduced an idea of simple beauty to
the domestic interior, noting, 'The white marble mantelpiece [has been] dismantled and sent to the churchyard'.

Morris was ahead of his time, but the generation of
designers, craftsmen and architects which followed in his
wake helped to bring his basic approach to a wider, more
receptive audience. M. H. Baillie Scott (1865–1945) was
an architect much concerned with artistic reform, particularly as it applied to the ordinary house. He, too, was a
champion of the inglenook, plain brickwork hearths, oak
mantel beams, settles and all the other unpretentious

adjuncts of the traditional country fireside, dating from
an era 'when the art of homemaking was so well understood'. The 'coarsely modelled', mass-produced grate was
rejected in favour of the wrought-iron dog grate, the
showy overmantel replaced by a simple shelf for willow
pattern plates. 'So much of the comfort as well as the
beauty of a room depends on a well-arranged fireside that
few will underrate its importance,' he wrote.

The founder of the Guild and School of Handicrafts,
C. R. Ashbee (1863–1942), designed cast-iron fireplaces
with integral grates and hoods to bring a new refinement
of ornament to mass production. Inset with copper or
brass, these elegant designs were intended to be painted
black, white or to co-ordinate with the main colour of the
wall decoration.

Sir Edwin Lutyens and C. F. A. Voysey were other
influential architects who brought an awareness of earlier
traditions to their designs. For the library at Knebworth
House, Lutyens designed a plain oak chimneypiece inset

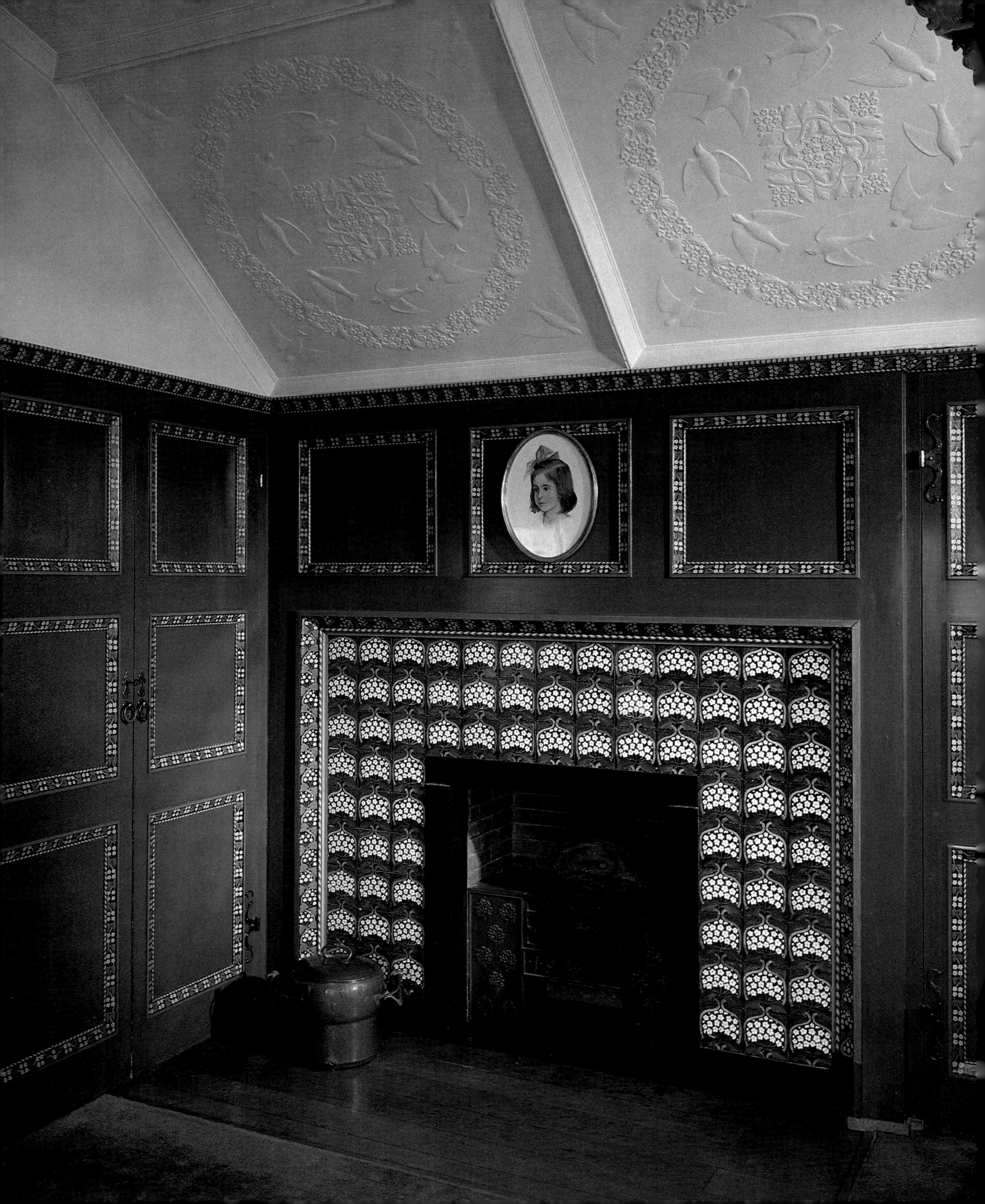

ABOVE *Richard Norman Shaw (1831–1912) was a leading figure in the creation of the 'Old English' style popular towards the end of the nineteenth century. Flete, Devon, was rebuilt by Shaw, assisted by W. R. Lethaby, between 1877 and 1883 for banker H. B. Mildmay. A late-medieval fireplace with flanking quatrefoil columns was reused in this room.* RIGHT *A simple bedroom fireplace at Ayr Mount, North Carolina, has a plain panelled wood surround roughly washed in grey-blue to match the window frame and dado.*

with a marble roundel. Libraries, billiard rooms and the newly reintroduced great hall were all popular locations for this sober, no-nonsense style. The hall fireplace seemed to call for a special architectural solution, in keeping with its ancestry.

Current in the final decades of the nineteenth century was another style related to the vernacular Gothic, the 'Queen Anne', or 'Shingle' style in its American variation.

ARTISTIC REFORM

M. H. Baillie Scott condemned the mass-produced fireplace in THE FIREPLACE OF THE SUBURBAN HOUSE:

I N THE AVERAGE HOUSE THE treatment of the fireplace is painfully ugly, and the coarsely modelled cast-iron grate, with its mantelpiece of enamelled slate, are things which one can only try to obliterate with drapery, while the stock overmantel with its bevelled mirrors and flimsy construction is hardly less objectionable.

BELOW *An interior scheme by Baillie Scott from 1901. The fireplace with its gleaming copper hood, deep blue tiles and Art Nouveau detail, is an integral feature of the scheme. The hearth is flanked by built-in cupboards and shelving. Baillie Scott's work was much admired in Europe, especially in Germany.*

OPPOSITE *'Hide and Seek' by Carl Larsson (1855–1919). The Larsson family spent summers at a country cottage near Falun, Sweden, where Larsson recorded many such charming scenes. The collected illustrations, published in book form, helped to popularize the light, colourful and unpretentious style of decorating he loved.*

Picturesque, informal, asymmetrical and, above all, comfortable, the Queen Anne style summarized an entire approach to traditional decor rather than copying any particular feature or period. Its enthusiasts were the better-off middle classes, with a yearning for the countryside and a more casual approach to living than their forebears. Lighter colours, faded chintz, a sympathetic blend of old and new, a tolerance of wear and tear, were all hallmarks of this style: elements we can now see today as the origins of 'country style'. Also known as 'Free English', it provided the context in which innovative designers such as Voysey worked. The Orchard, Chorleywood (1899), by Voysey featured a fireplace of astonishing simplicity: the plain tiled surround framed a narrow opening and the mantelshelf aligned with the picture rail.

The new country houses built around the turn of the century often included an inglenook in the dining room or library, while a more formal style still reigned in the drawing room. Inglenook hearths were generally constructed of plain brick, with beaten copper framing the opening and forming an overhanging hood. Despite the fact that these fireplaces were all coal-burning, freestanding dog grates and sturdy andirons were reintroduced as fire furniture, while the hob grate was revived in fireplaces of 'Queen Anne' style. (Neither could be regarded as progressive steps, either for heat efficiency or smoke control.) Wooden chimneypieces, with recesses to display pottery and plates, tiled panels, oak settles on either side of the recess, and small windows set into the flanking walls were all aspects of the revived inglenook. Some kind of inscription, often a homely motto, was a common feature of these hospitable firesides.

A watered-down version of the same aesthetic appeared in the last part of the nineteenth century and

RIGHT *The essence of country style: a farmhouse kitchen with stone floor, scrubbed pine table, baskets, Windsor chairs, and, of course, wide country hearth. This eighteenth-century fireplace has been updated by the addition of a stove to lend domestic comfort and convenience to a traditional room.*

OPPOSITE *Castle Drogo, Devon (1910–30) designed by Sir Edwin Lutyens for Julius Drewe, a tea merchant, is a grand, stark house largely built of granite. This massive granite fireplace accentuates the thickness of the walls and the austerity of the design: a striking modern interpretation of medieval English building. Drewe insisted on the castle form and specified that the walls be authentically six-feet deep.*

early years of the twentieth in the form of 'cosy corners'. Sometimes the effect was achieved simply by partitioning off a section of the drawing room with a screen, usually of open fretwork. If old marble or slate fireplaces could not be removed, they were painted to give them a more homely appearance; instead of elaborate drapery, there would be a simple, frilled, cretonne valance. This attempt at cottage-style conviviality, with the attendant wooden fireplaces, plain glazed bricks and copper hoods, was a far cry from the heavily laden and slavishly ornate chimney-pieces of half a century earlier.

Of course, nineteenth-century inglenooks or cosy corners, as they featured in country and suburban homes, were an idealization of a past style, rather than true structural components of the house. But, in the use of simple 'honest' materials and acknowledgement of the hearth as a focus of domestic intimacy, the inglenook had a significant impact on the way people came to view their

homes. Re-establishing the vernacular as a heritage worth preserving, the founders of the Arts and Crafts movement and the later designers in the Queen Anne idiom steered popular taste away from an ostentatious display of status towards a less pretentious appreciation of time-honoured country traditions. Morris's 'golden rule': 'Have nothing in your houses which you do not know to be useful or believe to be beautiful', encapsulates this approach.

Modern country style, then, owes something to rustic traditions of farmhouse and cottage, the craft ethic of the Morris interior, as well as the shabby gentility of turn-of-the-century Queen Anne. Transcending national boundaries and design epochs, country style is a powerful antidote to the complexities of modern life. It has probably been responsible for maintaining interest in the working fireplace. After all, who could imagine a country home without a hearth?

CHAPTER 6

REVIVAL AND RENEWAL

❈❈❈

DRAMATIC ADVANCES IN TECHNOLOGY have been the hallmark of the twentieth century. With the widespread availability of central heating, burning 'clean' modern fuels such as gas, oil and electricity, the open fire is no longer the hub of daily life. Between the two World Wars, new movements in design signalled the changes in society by promoting a pared-down aesthetic, stripping away decorative conventions established for centuries. The machine age demanded that the house should be 'a machine for living in', in Le Corbusier's famous phrase. As a relic of bygone days and antiquated technology, fireplaces seemed no longer relevant; for the first time in many thousands of years, the open fire almost disappeared.

But this is not the end of the story. Many people did not find the brave new interior entirely comfortable or sympathetic. 'Period features', once so enthusiastically abandoned during the course of modernization, were newly appreciated as a means of achieving some continuity with the past. In the last few decades, as this spirit of conservation has taken hold, the fireplace has made a triumphant comeback, restored to its rightful place at the heart of the home.

THE FALL AND RISE OF THE OPEN FIRE

At the turn of the century very little appeared to have changed on the domestic front. The Edwardian interior was lighter, brighter and somewhat less cluttered than its Victorian counterpart. In the words of Osbert Sitwell, 'The mantelshelf with all its fringed apparatus of red flannel globules and stalactites was delivered up to the lumber-room, while the chimney-piece beneath was now allowed once more to proclaim an unashamed nudity.'

OPPOSITE *The elemental form of this bold fireplace in a London townhouse makes a stark, sculptural focal point in a modern room. The rough finish, which acts as an effective counterpoint to the simplicity of the two square openings, is in stucco-antico, a traditional Italian stucco technique. The architectural purity of the whole composition is enhanced by minimal decoration.*

LEFT *A romantic bedroom in the Parisian townhouse where Alexandre Dumas wrote* The Three Musketeers *is furnished and decorated in a nineteenth-century interpretation of Louis XV style. The flowing curves of the marble fireplace are echoed in the lines of the bed and balanced by the large sheet of overmantel mirror. This room was once the studio of director Jean Renoir, son of the painter.*

RIGHT *The drawing room fireplace at Hill House, Helensburgh (1902–3), was designed by Charles Rennie Mackintosh (1868–1928) for W. R. Blackie. Mackintosh was responsible for every detail of the house. The beautiful all-white drawing room features a steel-framed fireplace faced in mosaic. The gesso panel above is by Margaret Macdonald, Mackintosh's wife. There are low seats at either side and built-in recesses to house decorative objects, all elegantly conceived.*

OPPOSITE *The dining room at Hill House is panelled in dark oak, a sombre colour scheme intended to focus attention on the dining table and table settings. The graphic fireplace is beautifully detailed and integrated within the panelling, with minimal Art Nouveau style decoration.*

With the ready availability of servants, there was no pressing need to abandon the cosy familiarity of the open fire. In the United States, where domestic staff had always been scarce, progress was already well underway in developing the labour-saving technologies which would transform domestic work.

The first of the progressive design movements of the twentieth century was Art Nouveau. This sinuous, organic style, which achieved its greatest prominence in European capitals such as Vienna, Brussels and Paris, had some impact on the decorative aspects of fireplace design. Cast-iron surrounds, andirons and fireplace furniture were ideally suited to the display of curvaceous plant and flower forms and provided a simple means of giving the fireplace a fashionably modern look. Inset tiles were also produced in a range of recognizably Art Nouveau motifs, notably stylized flower and leaf shapes.

A more radical approach to fireplace design can be seen in the work of Charles Rennie Mackintosh (1868–1928), whose short but brilliant career had a powerful influence on European designers. Like Voysey, Mackintosh treated the fireplace as an integral element in the composition of the entire wall, redefining proportions and refining ornament. With elongated mantelpieces and an emphasis on details such as niches and recesses, the geometric

precision of this style foreshadowed the mimimalism of the Modern movement. Mackintosh did not reject decoration, but used it in a subtle, sparing way. The fireplace in the library at Hill House, Helensburgh (1901), is set into a shallow, curved recess and features a mosaic surround inset with five drop-shaped panels. Both ends of the long, thin mantelpiece merge elegantly with the top shelves of flanking niches.

However, it was not until after the cataclysmic upheaval of the First World War that a more comprehensive redefinition of the interior came about. Women left domestic service, with its poor pay and long hours, for better working conditions in factories and offices. Middle-class households had to manage with substantially fewer staff and had to improve facilities to keep the servants they had. Suddenly, the open coal fire, with all the labour it entailed, became less attractive.

Predictably, the first open fires to go were on the upper levels. Gas fires installed in bedrooms did away with the chore of heaving heavy coal skuttles upstairs and freed the few remaining servants for more important tasks. In more public rooms, however, the gas fire was less socially acceptable and open fires remained.

With the widespread availability of electricity, the electric bar fire became a practical alternative to the

RIGHT A *living room designed by Hans Heller from* Moderne Bauformen *(c. 1910). Art Nouveau was a style that could easily be expressed in interior and architectural details, notably fireplaces. Defined by bold planes of colour, this hooded fireplace dominates the decor of the room.*

OPPOSITE An *overmantel composed of individual sheets of mirror reflects the delicate decoration of a coved ceiling, emphasizing the unusual architectural character of the room.*

gas fire. In the most rigorously modern settings, the bar fire was simply set into the wall, a forthright display of functional honesty. Others were framed by tiled or mirrored surrounds for a more luxurious look. Stepped tiled surrounds in ziggurat profiles were a feature of Art Deco fireplaces, while the characteristic 1940s suburban hearth was tiled in a subdued beige on top of a cast concrete base. The radical influence of modern design

THE END OF THE FIRE?

No room for the fireplace in this modern Bauhaus scheme, described by Josef Albers in 1924:

THERE IS NOTHING HERE which makes work and interferes with an impression of clarity: there are no sectional sofas or bedside tables, no sideboards or buffets, no cabinets, chandeliers, ball feet, mouldings, profile boards, cornices, ornaments, patterns, curtains, blinds, or knick-knacks.

can be detected in long, low fireplaces with minimal detail and decoration. In these horizontal compositions, the mantelshelf often extended to include low-level bookcases flanking the fire. A more vernacular look was provided by the brick-arched fireplace.

Another World War accelerated social change. In Britain, the middle-class housewife suddenly found herself in sole charge of cooking, cleaning, washing . . . a thousand and one domestic chores which she had neither the training nor the inclination to tackle. The booming economy of the 1950s enabled a new generation to modernize, improve and equip their homes with the latest consumer goods and services.

In 1944, 40 million tons of coal were still burned in Britain, accounting for half the air pollution and giving off enough smoke from domestic fires to ensure London's reputation for fog went undiminished. These fogs, familiar now only as the atmospheric backdrops to cinematic action, were deadly. They could last for days, even weeks, and on occasion were so dense that theatre performances had to be cancelled and traffic accidents proliferated. Peasoupers caused more than inconvenience. Air quality was so bad that deaths from related chest complaints soared. Four thousand people died as a result of the smog

RIGHT *A simple narrow fireplace in the bedroom of Virginia Woolf's home, Monk's House, features tiles hand-decorated by the artist Vanessa Bell.*

OPPOSITE A *post-modern fireplace in the New House, Wadhurst, by the architect John Outram. Balanced by floor-to-ceiling bookshelves, the fireplace with its rounded surround and deep overmantel framing a portrait forms the focus of a contemporary interior.*

of December 1952, a monstrous total that spurred legislation to clean the air.

The Clean Air Acts of 1955 and 1956 stipulated new, smokeless zones where only approved fuels, such as anthracite and coke, could be burned. Grants were eventually made available to convert old fireplaces to the new types of fuel. Meanwhile, more and more householders were installing central heating; new homes built in the 1960s and 1970s often had no fireplaces at all. In older properties, the drive to modernize saw fireplaces taken out, openings bricked up and plastered over. Generations that followed would see the relentless removal of dados, picture rails, cornices, ceiling roses, not to mention fireplaces, as mindless architectural vandalism. But at the time, such a stripping away and paring down reflected new concepts of interior space, initiated by progressive architects and designers in the 1930s and now gaining a wider currency.

Architects such as Le Corbusier and the radical designers of the prewar Bauhaus saw the house in terms of the functions it fulfilled. Superfluous ornament and decoration were abhorred. Fireplaces were irrelevant; warmth could be better provided by efficient central heating systems. Yet in British houses built during the 1930s in this idiom, the open fire was harder to cast aside. The December 1936 edition of the *Architectural Review*, an issue devoted to the Modern English House, featured a variety of Modernist houses that nevertheless included open fires in living rooms. 'The most important zone [in the living room] is that for sitting, and this, in spite of the efficiency of central heating, is usually planned, for sentimental reasons, round an open fuel-burning fireplace. This does not mean,' the editors sternly added, '...that the design need be reminiscent of those monumental marble and cast-iron erections beloved by our forefathers.'

Needless to say, the Modernist fireplace was far from sentimental in design. Sunken hearths, graphically plain openings and slate, marble, tile or reconstituted stone surrounds echoed the play of geometries in these severely minimal interiors. Shelves and cupboards were often integrated into the fireplace design, forming a low, horizontal band across the room. There was no clutter of knick-knacks to mark the domestic focus, merely 'a synchronized electric clock' to 'record continuous Greenwich time'.

The International Style which grew out of the Modern movement was a powerful influence on the postwar interior. Scandinavian Modern, a more domestically acceptable version based on similar principles, popularized a return to natural materials and surfaces, which could be expressed in exposed brick or stone fireplace surrounds. As central heating became more commonplace, and then a standard amenity, partitions were removed and walls taken down to open out the house into a sequence of linked spaces. Open-plan living, with its multi-purpose areas catering for all the activities of modern domestic life, was made possible by even, controllable levels of heating.

Despite all the comfort and convenience that we now take for granted in the home, the last few decades have seen a loss of confidence in Modernism and a return to traditional ways of decorating. The featureless character of the purpose-built suburban house and the strangely denuded appearance of properties converted in the rush to modernize provide a graphic illustration of the importance of some form of definition and detail in the interior. After only ten or fifteen years out of favour, 'period' details are back, lovingly replaced in their original settings. Architectural salvage firms have boomed, supplying new owners of old homes with the correct bits and pieces for restoration. Another growth industry is

OPPOSITE *The fireplace as domestic altar or shrine is displayed in this bold design statement, which makes conscious reference to classical precedent.*

LEFT *Wychcombe Studios, designed by the London-based American architect Rick Mather, reveals a modernist delight in the play of pure sculptural form. Here the fireplace is no more than a black rectangle set in the smooth face of the wall.*

architectural theft. A fireplace that would have been discarded in a builder's skip twenty years ago is now a covetable prize. In the late 1980s an Adam fireplace worth £30,000 made the headlines when it was stolen, but many more less valuable features regularly disappear from unsupervised building sites.

Today, most people want a fireplace in their home. Not necessarily in every room, but certainly in the living room, at the heart of the house where people gather. An American survey of new home-owners discovered that an estimated 90 per cent of their respondents looked for a home with a fireplace, even those living in areas where hard winters are unknown. New forms of grate and inset designs enable modern fireplaces to function as efficient supplementary sources of heating, a practical consideration given additional urgency by energy crises, power failures and ecological concerns. 'Zero-clearance' fires, consisting of highly insulated metal shells and flues, can be installed easily in modern homes without chimneys, even next to combustible walls.

Practicalities aside, the fireplace, it seems, remains as strongly identified with home as it ever was. An infinitely better focal point than a television, a graceful architectural flourish in a period room, an opportunity for individual expression, the fireplace has survived the whims of fashion to bring new light and cheer for years to come.

TERRORS OF THE NIGHT

In 1763 James Boswell recorded how he accidentally snuffed out his candle at two o'clock one morning. As the fire had died, he was forced to make his way to the kitchen to look for the tinder box:

UT THIS TINDER BOX I COULD not see, nor knew where to find. I was now filled with gloomy ideas of the terrors of the night.

RESTORING AND RENOVATING FIREPLACES

RESTORING THE FIREPLACE

Restoring a fireplace can vary in complexity and scope from a minor repair job to full-scale building work. If the intention is to restore the use of the fire as well as its opening, some specialist help will probably be required. In such cases, it is important to be aware that what is being restored is not merely an architectural feature, but a constructional system which has implications for insulation, ventilation and, of course, safety.

OPENING UP

Converted Victorian and Georgian properties have often been subject to sad 'improvements' where fire surrounds have been taken away and fireplaces boarded up. In these houses, with their wide chimney breasts forming more or less unalterable structural elements, it is generally easy to detect where the fireplace would have been and some vestige of it may well remain in the form of a fixed mantelshelf. A fireplace that has simply been boarded up and painted over is the easiest restoration prospect. Removing a board or panel and any interior wooden framework may well reveal a perfectly intact original cast-iron surround, although it is less common to find original tilework still *in situ*.

More comprehensive conversion will usually have involved bricking up the opening and plastering over the top. In these circumstances, an air brick to ventilate the chimney may have been installed. By removing such a vent or air brick it may be possible to assess the size of the original opening; alternatively a couple of bricks can be removed from the centre of the chimney breast about a foot from the floor. Because the chimney breast is a structural element, care must be taken not to weaken it

by undermining lintels or supporting beams on which the chimney breast rests. Although it is not difficult to clear away a bricked-up opening, specialist help is always advisable if it is not clear how far to proceed.

SAFETY AND MAINTENANCE

Regular maintenance is essential when a fireplace is in frequent use.

* Ensure the hearth and recess are free from cracks or damage.
* Inspect the flue for cracks and obstructions.
* Ensure the chimney is soundly constructed and leadwork flashings are intact.
* Sweep the chimney twice a year, before the first fire of the season, and after the last.
* Don't vary the type of fuel without taking advice.
* Only burn approved fuels in smokeless areas and never burn unseasoned wood.
* Never leave children unsupervised in rooms with open fires or stoves; fit secure fire-guards and keep matches, fire-lighting and all combustible materials out of reach.
* Always use a mesh firescreen to prevent sparks and cinders flying out onto the floor. Dense mesh screens are essential for wood-burning fires, as they may continue to burn well into the night.
* Bank fires down before retiring to bed by raking to the back. Prop logs upright in the rear corners so they cannot fall over.
* Keep a fire extinguisher in the home and fit smoke alarms.

The recognizable pattern of the average terraced house leaves little doubt as to the probable size and location of former fireplaces. But in farmhouses and cottages with a long history of adaptation, restoring an original hearth can involve more detective work. A central chimney and back-to-back fireplaces on the axis of the house plan may indicate the presence of an old inglenook; it is not unusual for such features to be buried under successive layers of brick. Wide inglenook fireplaces were often filled in at a later date to reduce the size of the opening and decrease draughts; renovation may well bring the full extent of such a hearth to light. Again, the structural ramifications of such work mean that specialist help is almost certainly necessary.

THE WORKING FIREPLACE

If you intend to use the fireplace, rather than simply renovate and display the opening, there are a number of elementary checks and safeguards that need to be performed. Once the opening has been cleared of debris and infilled brickwork, the next step is to investigate the condition of the flue and chimney.

When fireplaces are blocked off, the flue has often been plugged as well to reduce down-draughts. A blanket or old coat can sometimes be felt obstructing the throat

The epitome of between-the-wars chic, this scheme for a sitting room in a town flat was designed by Ambrose Heal, the innovative London retailer. Black moulding gives a crisp, graphic quality to the design.

of the flue and should be easy enough to remove. If there are no other detectable obstructions, you can test the draw of the flue by lighting the end of a rolled up newspaper and holding it underneath: if the smoke goes straight up, the draught is good; if it fills the room, there may be a number of causes, including blockages further up.

Old flues which have remained unused for long periods need to be inspected professionally to ensure that they are sound. The inner lining of the flue may deteriorate with age or the effects of wind, rain and frost, and sparks escaping through resulting cracks constitute a serious fire risk. A specialist can carry out a smoke test to see whether the flue is intact. The traditional method consists of sealing off the top of the chimney with a damp plug of sacking or rags and lighting a smoky fire in the fireplace. Special powders add scent or colour to the smoke to make

LUCKY SWEEP

EVERYONE KNOWS THAT GOOD luck rubs off if you shake hands with a sweep, but there are many other superstitions, too. Simply having a sweep cross the threshold was believed to be lucky; if you didn't shake his hand, you could always touch his collar for luck. And it was particularly fortunate for a wedding party if the bride was kissed by a sweep. In the old days, those who crossed a sweep's path would lick their finger and draw a cross on the toe of their boot, while the sight of the brush popping out of the chimney pot guaranteed good fortune.

it easier to detect. With all openings thoroughly screened, any smoke which escapes into rooms or externally will indicate a problem. Defective flues will need to be relined.

Thorough sweeping is essential before the fireplace is put back into use. Vacuum sweeping is adequate for regular maintenance, but brushes and rods are still the best way of dislodging obstructions, such as birds' nests, which may clutter up the flue or chimney pot. Sweeping may also reveal constructional problems such as awkward bends around which inflammable deposits of soot accumulate. In serious cases, the entire structure may need an overhaul before it is safe to use. Once the fire is in working order, the chimney should be swept at least twice a year, before the first and after the last fire of the season.

Smoky fires may also result if the flue opening is too high or too large. Air vents or grilles let into the walls or floor of the fireplace can help to improve the draught if the fire opening is large or the room is not adequately ventilated; double glazing and efficient modern insulation do not provide the right conditions for successful open fires. If masking around the surround with a cardboard framework reduces the smoke considerably, the opening can be reduced by installing an overhanging hood or canopy, by raising the hearth, or by filling in the opening as required. A baffle fitted across the opening, made of metal or glass, is often very effective. The recommended flue size is about one-eighth of the fireplace opening. Inserting a metal register or smoke hood to restrict flue size may be the answer, especially for wide inglenook openings.

The hearth should be made out of stone or concrete faced with tile and extend into the room to prevent flooring catching alight: a broken hearth is a significant fire risk. The size, extent and thickness of new hearths are controlled by building regulations and if there are any major repairs or alterations it is always advisable to seek professional guidance. You should also ensure that the recess is properly fireproofed. Original firebricks may need to be filled with fire cement if they have cracked. American wood-burning fireplaces are generally fitted with some form of dense mesh screen to guard against sparks flying out onto the floor, while modern flues include a 'damper' to seal in warm air when the fireplace is not in use.

A simple eighteenth-century fireplace framed in pine panelling in a house in London's Spitalfields, demonstrates a sympathetic approach to conservation. Originally, the panelling would have been painted; here it is left exposed for a warm, honey-coloured background.

In country areas, the chimneys of old houses may need special attention. Many chimneys were built to inordinate heights in an attempt to overcome smoke problems or escape the effect of neighbouring buildings or trees; others may simply have become wobbly or unstable with age and weathering. If the chimney is sound, but the fireplace continues to smoke, a chimney terminal, such as a cowl, may cure a persistent down-draught. Fitting wire mesh over the chimney pot or opening is a good idea if birds' nests are a regular problem. Mesh screens fitted to the tops of chimneys can also protect against sparks from a wood-burning fire alighting on neighbouring structures.

RENOVATING AND REPLACING OLD FIREPLACES

Existing surrounds that have been covered up or long disused generally require a degree of renovation to restore them to their former glory. It was common practice to obliterate such features with paint where they could not easily be removed; missing elements need sensitive replacement with designs that are sympathetic in character, material and scale.

All renovation work requires care. Uninformed or over-enthusiastic stripping can damage underlying finishes and materials and those in search of strict authenticity should be aware that original pine or plaster chimney-pieces were always intended to be painted, and removing old finishes may bring a surface to light that does not bear the scrutiny. Painting wooden or slate fireplaces in simulation of other, more expensive materials such as marble or hardwood was common practice (and vice versa: marble was sometimes painted to give it a home-lier appearance); if the surround is warm to the touch, it

A bathroom installed in an eighteenth-century room boasts an original fireplace, accentuated by painted wall panels of classical fragments created by Argentine artist Riccardo Cinalli.

BUILDING A WOOD FIRE

*Use only three to four logs.
*Place the largest, preferably of hardwood, to the back to act as a back log or back brand.
*Place another log at the front.
*Fill the space between the front log and back log with kindling, newspaper, small sticks or twigs.
*Place one or two logs over the top.
*Open the damper, if there is one, and light the fire. Once the kindling has burned and the logs have caught, push them together with a poker.
*Leave the fire alone, adding a log at a time as it burns down.
*Keep the ashes at a depth of about two inches.

may well not be marble but wood painted to look like it. Many Georgian 'composite' fireplaces have also been ruined by indiscriminate use of solvent which dissolves the actual material; applied plaster or gesso decoration can be damaged by scraping. When using any proprietary stripper, it is essential to test on a small area first to assess the effect.

Marble chimneypieces stain and discolour easily, which is why many have been given a cosmetic coat of paint. When white marble fireplaces fell from fashion at the end of the nineteenth century, it was also common to disguise such features with paint. Marble can be brought back to its original finish with the careful application of a commercial marble cleaner: never use household bleach. Use a chemical stripper to remove paint. Warm soapy water is adequate for light soiling; fuller's earth or other absorbent natural cleansers can be applied to areas with ingrained stains. There are also special marble polishes or waxes for a final protective layer.

Wooden chimneypieces, especially those with fine carved detail clogged with layers of paint, also demand careful stripping by hand. Chemical strippers are best; burning off paint can easily damage the detail. Follow manufacturer's instructions and ensure that the solvent has had adequate time to work before easing off the old paint with a scraper. Work into corners and crevices with old toothbrushes.

Cast-iron fireplaces were often painted, either black, white or to co-ordinate with the room decoration. Stripping can be done professionally. Tiles, a feature of so many late nineteenth-century cast-iron fireplaces, may also be disfigured by paint or dirt. They can be washed with distilled water and detergent for superficial cleaning. To remove paint, tiles should first be soaked with water and then stripped with water-based stripper. To replace missing, broken or badly cracked tiles, it is usually necessary to remove the fireplace. In Victorian cast-iron surrounds, tile panels are set into the splayed sides, fixed into position with plaster. Replacement or mended tiles should be slotted into the framework and replastered in place.

When the fire surround is entirely missing, replacements can be found from a number of sources. Salvage firms and junk yards stock a range of original surrounds from different periods, from plain cast-iron all-in-one fireplaces to marble panels for assembly on site. New fireplaces of simple design can be commissioned from builders; reproductions of basic period patterns are also widely available, although these rarely match the finesse of original specimens. The district archive department may be able to supply information enabling your house to be dated precisely, which helps if you are interested in achieving authenticity. Another solution is to investigate similar houses in the vicinity to discover if any retain original details, and then commission a copy from a craftsman.

More important than a slavish attention to period detail, however, is matching the fireplace to the room in terms of proportion and level of ornamentation. A richly elaborate surround that dominates the wall will be overpowering in a room of ordinary dimensions; on the other hand, a small, plain surround will be wildly out of character in a high-ceilinged space with grand mouldings.

Before the surround is fixed, it is necessary to consider the type of grate you will require. In an old, wide hearth, free-standing grates are appropriate. Those with integral cast-iron firebacks provide additional protection for the back of the hearth. Smaller Victorian or Edwardian openings with narrow-throated flues were designed to be fitted with cast-iron register grates that form an inner skin to the opening. (The register is an adjustable aperture, flap or damper to regulate air flow to the fire.) It may be difficult to ensure a perfect fit, but the opening can be adjusted with brick infill or concrete lintel so that the grate fits snugly. The front plate of the grate should be stuck to the wall with fire cement. Then the area between the grate and the back wall of the hearth should be filled with fire cement or lightweight concrete, applied through the damper. The top of the filling should slope slightly from the opening up towards the wall.

The next step is to fit the surround. Wooden and cast-iron fireplaces are generally made to be fixed as a single unit. Wooden fireplaces with integral mantelshelves can be installed by attaching them to the wall with nails or screws fitted through special fixings on the jambs (side supports). Cast-iron fireplaces are similarly attached by screws through cast fittings at the top and bottom of the jambs. A separate mantelshelf may be bolted on.

Marble fireplaces come in sections: the jambs or side supports, the frieze or lintel, and the shelf. Marble is heavy and the individual components need to be fixed together and to the wall using a combination of fine casting plaster and metal ties and hooks. Unless you are utterly confident in your DIY skills, it is best to obtain specialist help.

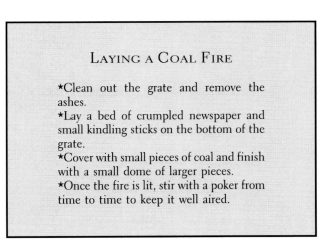

LAYING A COAL FIRE

*Clean out the grate and remove the ashes.
*Lay a bed of crumpled newspaper and small kindling sticks on the bottom of the grate.
*Cover with small pieces of coal and finish with a small dome of larger pieces.
*Once the fire is lit, stir with a poker from time to time to keep it well aired.

Despite the inconvenience of the open fire, the fireplace as focal point has proved hard to abandon. Here, in a 1933 living room designed by John Duncan Miller, the fireplace has been pared to the minimum and fitted with an electric bar fire. For all its efficiency, electric heating cannot be said to have quite the same appeal as firelight.

THE DECORATED FIREPLACE

No single element in the interior has such a defining impact as the fireplace. Seating arrangements radiate from hearthside comforts, the mantelshelf accumulates treasures and souvenirs, the chimney breast is the natural place for a bold decorative statement. The delicate modelling of an Adam-style surround enhances the refinement of a period room; a rustic stone hearth adds a rugged flavour to a wood-panelled den.

One of the most satisfying aspects of the fireplace is that it offers so much scope for individual expression. A host of decorating conventions are associated with the fireplace, traditional forms of arrangement and display that date from specific periods in the history of the interior. But design and decoration today are no longer rulebound and there is greater freedom than ever before for original flair and creativity.

As an architectural detail, the style of the fireplace can determine the character of the room. If you are interested in historical accuracy, then choosing a surround will involve a little research to determine the right style, material and treatment for the type of room and age of the house. But there is no need to be inhibited by history. Exciting contrasts of texture, design and colour can make a more dynamic contribution to a room. Many Victorians simply would not have countenanced a black

The elegance and sense of relaxed luxury of a Parisian salon is evoked in this London townhouse. A simple low relief surround frames a plain hearth; real flickering flames are wittily echoed in the papier-mâché sun medallion above. The golden glow from the fireplace is amplified in the yellow decoration, picked out with defining touches of crimson in the banding of the cupboard doors.

marble fireplace in a drawing room and would have shuddered at the prospect of leaving a cast-iron mantelpiece unpainted. Unblinkered by such interior etiquette, we are free to appreciate a broader range of materials and finishes.

In terms of decoration, the fireplace needs to be considered along with the treatment of the walls. It can be decorated to blend in with a basic colour scheme or to contrast with it. Wooden fireplaces painted the same colour as skirting boards and trim stand out as a form of graphic definition against different toned walls; in a painted panelled room, co-ordinating walls and fireplace accentuates the articulation of the surfaces. Classical fireplaces with fine detail look particularly crisp and elegant painted white, set off against delicately patterned or painted walls. If the fireplace is simple and plain, edging it with a tiled, stencilled or paper border can increase its visual importance. And there's plenty of scope for paint effects: marbling, spattering or graining can lift an unexceptional surround out of the ordinary and inject a dash of exuberance and wit.

It is instinctive to group furniture to reflect the fireside focus, even if in the modern living room the fireplace has to compete with the television as a point of interest. With a fireplace in the centre of a main wall, some form of symmetrical arrangement is natural, balancing sofas and chairs to create an equal weighting on both sides. Another basic pattern follows the tradition of the country hearth, with high-backed seating drawn up in a close circle around the fire. Modern hearths may offer the opportunity to build in seating in the form of a wide shelf to either side of the fire, creating cosy alcoves in which to curl up with a book.

At eye level as you enter the room, the mantelshelf is a natural place for display. Symmetrical sets of porcelain or 'garnitures' were created in the seventeenth and eighteenth centuries especially for mantelpiece display; by the late eighteenth century, ornaments were proliferating. The centrally placed chimney clock and flanking candlesticks also have a long association with the fireside; in recent times, printed invitation cards and family photographs have taken up residence.

One of the quickest ways of changing the focus of the room is to change what you put on the mantelpiece. Whatever your objects of desire, varying the collection from season to season helps to generate a sense of vitality and energy in your surroundings when other more basic elements cannot be so readily altered. Unite arrangements by colour, texture, type and then inject a contrast for a note of quirky irreverence. A row of candlesticks of staggered height looks romantic and theatrical, the light reflected in an overmantel mirror. Patterned plates or coloured glassware provide convivial accompaniments to a dining-room fireplace. Found objects – shells, fossils, washed beach stones – bring natural beauty to a rustic hearth.

The chimney breast has always had great decorative importance. Most fireplaces, unless the mantelpiece is treated in a particularly eye-catching or elaborate way, seem to require some form of balancing treatment above to match the bold punctuation point made by the opening itself. Mirror, pictures, busts on plinths, trophies, are all conventional ways of highlighting this area of wall. The main issue is one of scale. A small watercolour would look ridiculously lost over an ornate marble chimneypiece; a gilt overmantel mirror would dwarf a plain moulded surround.

At floor level, too, there is scope for display. Weathered stones, bowls, urns, plants, can be grouped to one side of the hearth, offsetting its symmetry. And in the summer months, when the fire is not in use, flower arrangements, plants or heaped fir cones, all create a living presence that dispels the blank cold look of an empty hearth.

LEFT A *present-day still-life arrangement on a nineteenth-century mantelpiece captures the mood of a typical artisan's home. At the bottom end of the social scale, there was often no money for decorative niceties and cut-out newspaper made a humble substitute for the traditional cloth mantel runner or valance. One way of economizing on fuel in poor households was to place a couple of bricks in the hearth: a primitive form of 'storage heating'.*

CHAPTER 7

THE CLOSED FIRE

❀❀❀❀

THE STOVE OR THE CLOSED FIRE HAS never quite enjoyed the same level of appreciation as the traditional open fireplace. Yet stoves are efficient, safe and warm, and they have a long history of use in many parts of the world. And their relative neglect is even more surprising considering how immensely decorative many examples can be.

Northern Europe is the traditional home of the stove. It was this pattern of heating that early emigrants took with them to North America and, by the nineteenth century, stoves were being produced in a wide variety of designs for many types of domestic situation. The only country to resist the advantages of the closed fire was Britain, where the cheerful sight of burning logs or glowing coals was always a powerful argument against experimenting with any other kind of heating.

Today, technological advances in the construction of the modern fireplace, which mean that fuel is consumed more efficiently and the harmful effects of pollution are minimized, have resulted in closed fireplace systems which blur the boundaries between the stove and the open fire. With glass-fronted doors that enable the psychological as well as the physical warmth of the flames to be appreciated, modern devotees of the fire can have the best of both worlds.

THE STOVE

The use of wood-burning stoves to heat the interior is a long-established practice in German-speaking areas, Russia and Scandinavia, northern regions with severe enough winters to make reliable heating a priority. Logs stacked in neat piles beside farmhouses are still a common sight in the colder areas of Europe. The first stoves, dating back around five hundred years, were made of brick or glazed tile, similar to the traditional German *Kachelofen*, which had a multi-purpose use for warming rooms, baking and heating water.

OPPOSITE *The drawing room in the poet and playwright Friedrich Schiller's eighteenth-century house in Weimar, Germany, was warmed by a Kachelofen, or stove, set in a corner niche. The stove, made of terracotta and cast-iron, is in the form of a classical column topped with an urn, an elegant addition to the neoclassical surroundings.*

LEFT *These highly colourful and decorative stoves are German in origin and were illustrated in* Das Buch der Efindungen, 1896. *Stove designs were often extremely elaborate and architecturally inspired. Despite their obvious aesthetic and practical qualities, the British never adopted this form of heating with any enthusiasm.*

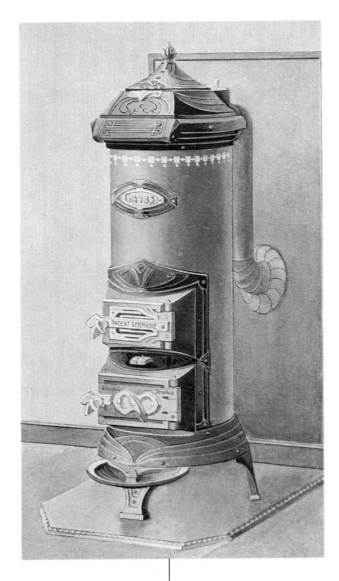

RIGHT *This German stove was produced in 1909. It stands on a heat-resistant plate and is vented by a flue at the rear.*

OPPOSITE *The octagonal dining room at Sturehov Manor, Sweden, dates from the late eighteenth-century. The glazed ceramic columned stove, enriched with neoclassical detail, was made near Stockholm. Some stoves that were set in niches could be fed from the rear via a wall opening into an anteroom, which meant that servants did not need to enter the main apartment to perform this duty.*

By the fifteenth and sixteenth centuries, stoves were generally faced in glazed tiles. These tiles, which proved to conduct heat well, were moulded in relief and lead-glazed in a limited number of colours, usually green and black, later brown and yellow. The generic term for such stove tiles is Hafner-ware; the Hafner were the stove makers of Germany, Austria and Switzerland who established a number of important production centres, including Creussen, Nuremberg, Ravensburg, and Winterthur.

Unlike the open fire, the stove needed as airtight a room as possible to be effective. In fact, the various terms for stove – including 'stufa' and 'stew' – were applied to the room which contained the stove, a kind of heated chamber, as insulated from draughts as possible, where people gathered to keep warm on freezing nights. Doors and shutters closed tight, the large, bulky stove radiated warmth and heated the air. English travellers noted the Continental practice with more than a little disdain, paying special attention to the 'ill smells' of these closed, heated rooms. Whether the smells were the natural accompaniment of infrequently washed bodies steaming in the warmth of the room, or the result of inefficiently discharged gases from the stove itself, is not clear.

From the sixteenth century, stove tiles were also produced in tin-glazed earthenware. Known as *faïence* in France, Germany and Scandinavia, *maiolica* in Italy, delft in the Netherlands, this ceramic technique enabled pottery to be glazed opaque white and decorated in simulation of Chinese porcelain. Rouen in Normandy supplied blue and white *faïence* tiles for French stoves.

Most stoves have always been cylinder-shaped or rectangular, but during the height of the Rococo, more fanciful designs appeared, with sinuous curves and rich embellishment, suitable for display in the most fashionable apartments. The indefatigable English traveller Lady Mary Wortley Montagu, touring the Continent in the early eighteenth century, was liberal in her praise of the stoves she had seen, noting that they were not only highly efficient, but also quite magnificent. Shaped like porcelain jars or cabinets, painted and gilt, such items were more than a match for the splendours of a Rococo chimneypiece. Stoves also provided the heat for orangeries where exotic fruits were brought on to tempt the tastebuds of fashionable society.

When the influence of the Rococo waned and neoclassicism swept into fashion, ceramic stoves were produced in architectural forms. Designs from the late

RIGHT *The magnificent ballroom in the eighteenth-century Wittums Palais in Weimar features a cast- and sheet-iron stove in the suitably classical form of a plinth surmounted by an urn. The palace was one of the many residences of Princess Anna Amalia and the stove is typical of those found in German castles.*

eighteenth century incorporated columns, urns and other recognizable classical motifs. White cylindrical tiled stoves decorated with laurel wreaths and festoons were seen in Empire rooms all over Northern Europe.

Since the late seventeenth century, cast iron had begun to be used for stoves. Iron stoves, which radiated heat thirty times faster than those made of glazed earthenware, were taken by early emigrants to America, particularly the Pennsylvania Dutch (Deutsch). Homely and utilitarian, iron stoves lacked the beauty and elaboration of ceramic versions. It was soon discovered that the longer the stove pipe, the warmer the room and the slower the rate of combustion, which meant that fuel lasted longer. Lengths of angled flue pipe were equally incompatible with rooms of architectural pretension.

Benjamin Franklin (1706–90), famous for electrical experiments among many other endeavours, attempted to improve the appearance of the stove in one critical respect. Identifying its essential drawback, at least from a British point of view, Franklin noted that the stove offered 'no sight of the fire which is itself a pleasant thing'. His open stove, invented in 1745, had a double metal skin to enable warm air to be circulated inside, and was designed to sit under a chimneypiece.

The Franklin or Pennsylvania fireplace had certain admirers in England and Europe; the typical English hall stove of the eighteenth and nineteenth centuries was generally of a similar type. In the mid-eighteenth century, stoves were designed as part of the architectural fitting of a room. James Wyatt's designs for the dining room at Slane Castle featured alcoves fitted with stoves surmounted by classical figures holding lamps. In the

RIGHT *This gloriously elaborate 'Kitchener' – a closed cooking range from the nineteenth century – accommodated many different types of cooking from stewing to roasting, provided hot water for washing and heated flat irons. Such ranges were, however, difficult to keep clean and maintain, and some failed to function properly.*

OPPOSITE *Cast-iron stoves were a common means of heating ordinary houses and public places in North America. The cigar shape of this example reflects the fact that wood burns from front to back in a stove.*

same mode was an Adam design for a hall stove with an oil lamp on top, where the chimney was in the form of an obelisk. The Carron Ironworks, the foundry which produced grates to Adam's designs, also made stoves in the classical idiom, as did the Tula Ironworks in Russia.

Hall stoves were sometimes in the form of vases placed on pedestals, which warmed the air of draughty passageways and staircases. Even more elaborate disguises were occasionally adopted. Stoves concealed as trophies of arms heated the entrance passage at Belvoir. A hinged shield opened to reveal the fire, and pikes were manipulated to control the draught.

Aside from the stove's workaday appearance and lack of a visible fire, the other common complaint was that it dried the air and caused all sorts of maladies, from depression to weakness to 'iron cough'. Most English travellers to the United States in the nineteenth century commented unfavourably on the heat and dryness of the atmosphere indoors. Pot-bellied stoves glowing red hot were common in homes, schools and public places.

ONE OF THE CONVENIENCES OF LIFE

Lady Mary Wortley Montagu, writing to her sister, Lady Mar, from Blankenburg, Germany 17 December 1716:

I AM SURPRIZ'D WE DO NOT practise in England so usefull an Invention. This reflection naturally leads me to consider our obstinacy in shakeing with cold 6 months in the year rather than make use of Stoves, which are certainly one of the conveniencys of Life; and so far from spoiling the form of a Room, they add very much to the magnificence of it when they are painted and gilt as at Vienna, or at Dresden where they are often in the shapes of China Jars, Statues or fine Cabinets, so naturally represented they are not to be distinguish'd. If ever I return, in defiance of the Fashion, you shall certainly see one in [my] chamber....

OPPOSITE *The same stove features in one of Larsson's delightful representations of the family summer home, 'Young Boy Seated in an Interior'. Karin, Larsson's wife, was also an artist and they decorated and furnished their house together, using traditional Scandinavian handicrafts and designs.*

LEFT *This decorative tiled stove stands in the corner of the drawing room in Carl Larsson's summer house. Larsson found the stove, dated 1754, on a building site and in need of some repair. His neighbours thought him foolish for wanting to restore and use it.*

Standing on legs to protect the floor from fierce heat, most stoves were simple iron boxes or cylinders with vented hinged doors for feeding the fire and a small draught control. A vent directed smoke and gases up the chimney.

During the nineteenth century a host of different designs were produced, with increasing technical sophistication that facilitated temperature control and attempted to prevent overheating. The finest examples, decoratively speaking, featured nickel plating, sumptuous enamelled panels painted with scenes, ceramic tiles and pierced ironwork. To the English, however, they remained, in the words of Dickens, merely 'red hot monsters'.

With the arrival of modern central heating, the stove, like the open fire, seemed to have a minor role. But, just as the open fire had enjoyed a revival in recent years, the comforts of the wood-burning stove have also been

rediscovered, tinged, perhaps, with some nostalgia for the old cosy focus of country life.

A wide variety of designs, many of them Scandinavian or North American, are produced today, incorporating a range of sophisticated features in tune with modern demands for efficiency and safety. Completely airtight, with heat-resistant glass doors to provide a view of the fire, many modern stoves feature internal smoke baffles that move air around inside and prevent tar from building up, as well as thermostatic damper controls to maintain a set level of warmth. Blowers drive out warm air at the base of the stove so heat is not wasted. There are also reproductions of traditional designs for greater decorative interest.

INSTALLING A STOVE
A well-designed, modern, wood-burning stove is economical and efficient, supplying great levels of heat using only

OPPOSITE *The discreet functionalism of the modern stove has commended it to many architects and designers. In this contemporary house the polished flue from the stove is treated as a design element in itself, paired with the concrete structural column.*

LEFT *Charleston, a Sussex farmhouse, was a country retreat for artists and writers of the Bloomsbury Group and the home of Duncan Grant and Vanessa Bell. The drawing room fireplace is heated by a Pither stove. The surround is painted with figures by Duncan Grant in the exuberant decorative style that eventually embellished every surface in the house.*

six to ten logs a day. It is essential to research the market carefully to choose a stove that complies with safety regulations and it is generally advisable to have it installed professionally.

Standard recommendations are that a stove should be positioned no less than three feet from a combustible wall or ceiling and should stand on some kind of fireproof pad. Obviously, the further out into the room, the more efficient it will be at radiating heat, but care must also be taken to ensure that the stove is away from main routes around the house, since its surfaces become exceptionally hot.

Stove flues can be vented out of an existing chimney but the opening must be shut off completely. The base of the chimney should also be filled in with sand below the pipe connection to make cleaning easier. A well-designed stove with a well-insulated and tightly sealed pipe should burn hot enough to prevent any build-up of tarry deposits, which can constitute a fire hazard. But regular maintenance, proper installation and correct loading and burning procedures are all essential for safe use: follow manufacturer's instructions to the letter.

OTHER FORMS OF CLOSED FIRE

When you restore an old fireplace to working order, you also revive its inefficiencies. An open fire needs a good air supply, which basically means a draughty room. Double-glazing and the sound construction of modern homes do not provide the ideal conditions for open fires, and in a well-sealed room, fireplace fumes can build up to a dangerous level. At the same time, opening up a flue contributes to heat loss. Energy crises have brought a new

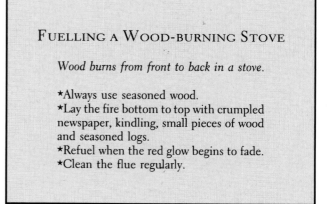

FUELLING A WOOD-BURNING STOVE

Wood burns from front to back in a stove.

*Always use seasoned wood.
*Lay the fire bottom to top with crumpled newspaper, kindling, small pieces of wood and seasoned logs.
*Refuel when the red glow begins to fade.
*Clean the flue regularly.

The modern wood-burning stove, which gives a comforting view of the blazing fire, restores the hearth to the heart of the home. In these up-to-date designs the line between fireplace and stove is blurred; highly insulated, efficient and safe, perhaps their greatest

attraction remains the age-old pleasure of watching a living fire. In this contemporary timber house on the Thames, the scale of the room is counteracted by the snug wooden panelling and the central wood stove.

awareness of the scarcity of the earth's resources, and the ecology movement has spelled out the dangers of contributing to global warming and acid rain.

The answer to at least some of these problems has come in the form of closed fireplaces. With complete combustion and circulating heat-exchange systems through elaborate ducting, very little fuel is wasted and pollution is minimized. Circulating fireplaces provide a useful supplement to standard methods of heating and, in some cases, even replace them.

In a revival of the old central hearth idea, there are free-standing fireplaces with prefabricated metal flues and overhanging hoods. A cross between a fireplace and a stove, most of these are designed to burn wood and

feature some form of enclosure, usually a glass door, which enables the fire to be seen but keeps sparks from flying onto the floor. Then there are the familiar, enclosed coal fires such as those by Parkray or Rayburn, which have back boilers to heat a system of radiators; these, too, have glass doors to preserve the essential connection with the living fire.

In these designs, the distinction between the stove and open fire becomes blurred. Some modern prefabricated fires can be used either closed or open; some can be adapted for different types of fuel. The great range of models in production and all their technical implications can be appreciated by consulting an advisory service which specializes in solid fuel heating.

SELECT BIBLIOGRAPHY

ARTS AND CRAFTS IN BRITAIN AND AMERICA, *Isabelle Anscombe and Charlotte Gere*, Academy Editions (1978)

AUTHENTIC DECOR, *Peter Thornton*, Weidenfeld and Nicolson (1984)

BELOW STAIRS IN THE GREAT COUNTRY HOUSES, *Adeline Hartcup*, Sidgwick and Jackson (1980)

THE BOOK OF HOUSEHOLD MANAGEMENT, *Isabella Beeton* (1861)

THE BRITISH KITCHEN, *Doreen Yarwood*, Batsford (1981)

A COMPLETE BODY OF ARCHITECTURE, *Isaac Ware* (1756)

THE COOK'S ROOM, ed. *A. Davidson*, HarperCollins (1991)

ENGLISH DECORATION IN THE 18TH CENTURY, *John Fowler and John Cornforth*, Barrie and Jenkins (1974)

THE ENGLISH FIREPLACE, *Nicholas Hills*, Quiller (1983)

THE ENGLISH TERRACED HOUSE, *Stefan Muthesius*, Yale University Press (1982)

THE FIREPLACE BOOK, *Roxana Macdonald*, Architectural Press (1984)

THE FIREPLACE IN THE HOME, *Trudy West*, David and Charles (1976)

FIREPLACES, *Kinkead/Edwards*, Chronicle Books (1992)

FROM KITCHEN TO GARRET – HINTS FOR YOUNG HOUSEHOLDERS, *J. E. Panton* (1890)

GEORGIAN GRACE, *John Gloag* (1956)

A HISTORY OF FIRE AND FLAME, *Oliver C. de C. Ellis* (1932)

HOME FIRES BURNING, *Lawrence Wright*, Routledge and Kegan Paul (1964)

HOW OLD IS YOUR HOUSE? *Pamela Cunnington*, Alpha Books (1980)

LIFE BELOW STAIRS, *F. E. Huggett* (1977)

LIFE IN THE ENGLISH COUNTRY HOUSE, *Mark Girouard*, Yale University Press (1978)

LONDON: THE ART OF GEORGIAN BUILDING, *Dan Cruikshank and Peter Wyld*, Architectural Press (1975)

THE NATURAL HOUSE BOOK, *David Pearson*, Conran Octopus (1989)

OBJECTS OF DESIRE, *Adrian Forty*, Thames and Hudson (1986)

OUR DOMESTIC FIREPLACES, *F. Edwards* (1865)

PERIOD DECORATING, *Mary Gilliatt*, Conran Octopus (1990)

VICTORIAN AND EDWARDIAN FURNITURE AND INTERIORS, *Jeremy Cooper*, Thames and Hudson (1987)

A WOMAN'S WORK IS NEVER DONE, *Caroline Davidson*, Chatto and Windus (1982)

APPENDIX

SOURCES

HISTORIC HOUSES

Many of the historic houses illustrated in this book are open to the public and well worth visiting to see original fireplaces in the settings for which they were designed. In Britain, many of these properties are owned and administered by the National Trust. For further information and details of opening times contact:
National Trust for Places of Historic Interest or Natural Beauty
36 Queen Anne's Gate
London SW1H 9AS

MUSEUMS

BRITAIN

The Brooking Collection
University of Greenwich
Oakfield Lane
Dartford
Kent DA1 2SZ
Reference collection of architectural detail, including grates, open by appointment. Large collection of period grates housed separately, which can also be viewed by arrangement.

Geffrye Museum
Kingsland Road
Shoreditch
London E2 8EA
A collection of English furniture and woodwork from 1600 to 1939, arranged in reconstructed room settings.

Victoria and Albert Museum
Cromwell Road
London SW7 2RL

Weald and Downland Museum
Singleton
West Sussex
Museum of early agricultural life, with reconstructed 15th-century farmhouse and central hearth.

UNITED STATES

Colonial Williamsburg
Goodwin Building
Williamsburg
Virginia 23185

Henry Francis du Pont Winterthur Museum
Winterthur
Delaware 19735

Metropolitan Museum of Art
Fifth Avenue at 82nd St
New York NY 10028

ADVICE

Building Centre
26 Store Street
London WC1E 7BT
Advice and information on building materials and products.

Crafts Council
44a Pentonville Road
London N1 9HF
An excellent source for locating craftspeople who create fireplaces and accessories to commission. The 'Index of Selected Makers' is a directory of recommended makers working in different media. Examples of work can be viewed on slide to facilitate choice. The information service also maintains a fully comprehensive National Register of Makers.

The Georgian Group
37 Spital Square
London E1 6DY
Advice and information on all aspects of Georgian building and Georgian taste. They publish a series of advisory leaflets called 'The Georgian Group Guides'. See number 9, 'Fireplaces'.

National Association of Chimney Sweeps
St Mary's Chambers
19 Station Road
Stone
Staffordshire ST15 8JP

National Fireplace Association
8th Floor
Bridge House
Smallbrook Queensway
Birmingham B5 4JP
Promotional association for the fireplace industry. Publishes an annual yearbook for potential customers, a range of technical leaflets, and a national directory of members. Invaluable source of information and consumer guidance on every aspect of the fireplace: fuels, chimneys, flues, linings, fireplaces, accessories, installation, stoves, safety, servicing and suppliers.

The Society for the Protection of Ancient Buildings
37 Spital Square
London E1 6DY
Advice on building history and repairs; information sheets available.

Solid Smokeless Fuels Federation
Devonshire House
Church Street
Sutton in Ashfield
Nottinghamshire NG17 1AE
Advice on use of solid smokeless fuels.

Victorian Society
1 Priory Gardens
London W4 1TT
Publish a series of advisory leaflets, 'Care for Victorian Houses', available by mail order. Particularly relevant are 'Fireplaces' (number 3 in the series) and 'Decorative Tiles' (number 2).

SOURCES
Acquisitions Fireplaces Limited
4–6 Jamestown Road
London NW1 7BY
Good range of reproduction mantels, inserts and accessories, in marble, wood and cast iron, based on traditional designs.

The Burning Question
19b Howe Street
Edinburgh EH3 6TE
Fire surrounds, stoves, fenders, tiles, accessories and overmantel mirrors. Installation service.

Craigavon Marble
Unit 9, Ulster Street Industrial Area
Ulster Street
Lurgan, Co Armagh
Northern Ireland
Carved marble surrounds based on classical designs.

Fireplace Designers Ltd
157c Great Portland Street
London W1
Contemporary and Art Deco surrounds in wood, marble and tile.

The Fireplace Shop
108–114 Glenthorne Road
London W6
Antique fireplaces from the 18th century to the present day; contemporary designs and fireplace accessories.

Franco-Belge UK
ACR Distribution
PO Box 70
Knowle
Solihull
West Midlands B93 0ET
Importers of French cast-iron stoves: wood-burning, gas and multifuel.

Hallidays Carved Pine Mantelpieces Ltd
The Old College
Dorchester-on-Thames
Oxon OX10 7HL
Leading specialists in hand-carved pine surrounds in the style of Adam and other 18th-century designers.

The London Architectural Salvage and Supply Company (LASSCO)
Mark Street
London EC2
Extensive range of original architectural fixtures, including fireplaces dating from the 17th, 18th and 19th centuries, as well as French 18th-century stone surrounds.

Marble Hill Fireplaces Limited
70–72 Richmond Road
Twickenham
Middlesex
French carved marble surrounds and modern reproductions.

Minster Fireplaces
Ilminster
Somerset TA19 9AS
Reconstituted stone fireplaces in traditional designs. Design and build service available.

Modus Design
16 The Warren
Radlett
Herts
Exciting and innovative modern fireplaces for the contemporary interior.

H. and E. Smith
Britannic Works
Broom Street
Hamley, Stoke-on-Trent
Staffordshire ST1 2ER
Decorative fireplace tiles.

Stonecraft Fireplaces
3 Lower London Road
Edinburgh EH7 5TJ
Marble, slate, granite and stone fireplaces in a range of simple designs. Cast-iron inserts.

Stovax Limited
Falcon Road
Sowton Industrial Estate
Exeter
Devon EX2 7LF
Authentic cast-iron fireplaces, surrounds, accessories and decorative tiles.

VCW International Ltd
1 Smyth Road
Bedminster
Bristol BS3 2BX
Importers of gas, wood-burning and multifuel stoves from the United States.

Vermont Castings
1 Smyth Road
Bristol BS3 2BX
Suppliers of wood-burning stoves. Many designs are approved by the Department of the Environment for use in smoke control areas.

Walcot Reclamation Yard
108 Walcot Street
Bath
Avon
Good selection of original fireplaces from the 17th, 18th and 19th centuries, with some earlier stone examples. Wide variety of Victorian surrounds, grates and cast-iron inserts.

INDEX

Page numbers in *italic*
refer to illustrations

PICTURE CREDITS: